# BACK HOME
## in Amite County, Mississippi

*To: John Robert write! Enjoy!*

## BILLY ANDERS

outskirts
press

# DEDICATION

"Without a past, there is no future."

This book is dedicated to the work of the Amite County Historical and Genealogical Society, founded in 2004 in Liberty, Mississippi, whose motto is above. That group works to "provide for the discovery, preservation, and dissemination of materials and knowledge, about the history of peoples, families, structures, objects, and items of interest, importance, and value, in relation to Amite County, Mississippi, and its vicinity."

Thank you for what you do!

# TABLE OF CONTENTS

# ACKNOWLEDGEMENTS

Thanks! To my wife, Cynthia, for tolerating my time at the computer.

To my niece, Emily Jefford, for important proofreading.

To readers of these stories originally published in the Wilk-Amite Record of Gloster, Mississippi, who encouraged me to publish them in book form.

To my typing teacher during 1961 at Istrouma High School, Baton Rouge, Louisiana, without whose brave effort I might still be using a quill.

Most of all, to the Good Lord who has blessed me beyond measure.

# FOREWORD

WARNING! Expecting an exciting adventure book? Read no further. Thanks for your purchase but consign this work to the bathroom for rainy day reading and purchase something by fellow Mississippian John Grisham or Clive Cussler. The only way this will keep you glued to your seat will be if you're already sweaty when you go in there.

This is mostly a simple book of nostalgia, what it's like for a country boy to grow up at least partially in Amite County, Mississippi – venture out into the big, cold world over more than 50 years - never losing sight of where home is – and return in some fashion after all that time. I suppose it's mostly a memoir.

Many "knocks" on Mississippi were encountered during my worldly walkabout, and I am puzzled by that. Yes, those days of the 1940s and 1950s were probably poor in some respects with regard to money or fancy school facilities. But I never felt disadvantaged. We had good families, good teachers who cared, good food, and a good God who gave us the capability to do anything we set our minds to. I believe that so strongly that my coming Back Home to purchase and publish the Wilk-Amite Record during 2011 and 2012 was because I felt I owed my "homefolks" something for all the good they did in launching me into that big world.

My children and grandchildren have never lived in Mississippi and this is also written so they might gain some insight into the way ole dad or grandpa grew up.

Change is inevitable and Amite County has changed some. It's still a great place to begin or spend time in the middle or the end. Whatever is left of me in that latter phase will rest in the Robinson Baptist Church cemetery in Peoria, (Amite County) Mississippi, along with others of my family.

Remnants of the "old days" still exist and are a pleasure to look at and share. I hope you enjoy the tour provided herein and some of the other oddball adventures picked up along the way. I salute Amite County, Mississippi, for all it means to me!

It is a good place.

*Chapter 1*

# SMALL TOWN MEMORIES

## GIVE ME LIBERTY!

WHERE'S YOUR HOMETOWN? They're important to us. They give us roots and a sense of belonging. Many times we gravitate back to our hometown. Been to yours lately? Are there relatives or friends you'd like to see? Perhaps you should plan a visit.

During a recent holiday trip to Louisiana to visit family, I made a quick trip to my hometown. May I introduce you?

Liberty, Mississippi, is a small country town. If Louisiana is a boot, Liberty is just above the shoelaces, across the state line about 15 miles. Population is about 700 fulltime persons.

In earlier years, around 1900, Liberty had a railroad, used

primarily to haul timber to market. Yellow pine. It was the Liberty White Railroad. It ceased operations in 1921. It traveled about 20 miles, and connected with the Illinois Central in McComb, Mississippi.

It had and still has a Little Red Schoolhouse. In the middle 1800's, Liberty had a girls' finishing school. During the Civil War, Federal troops burned all of the school but the small music building. The school's director was a reverend from New York State. A temporary reprieve was given while musical instruments were removed. The distraught educator looked on.

The Federal commander, about to give the order to torch that final building, recognized the pastor as a former classmate from New York. The order was never given. The Little Red Schoolhouse survived and lives to this day. An act of kindness and friendship in the chaos of war.

Some notable persons have lived in Liberty or spent substantial time there. Liberty was a jumping-off point for Texas territory before the time of the Alamo. Colonel William Travis and Jim Bowie, who both died during the siege of the Alamo, spent time in Liberty.

Ever used Borden's Condensed Milk? Gail Borden was an early resident, and perfected his technique of condensing milk there. This product led to the formation of the Borden Milk Company. The old Borden house is gone but I still remember seeing it as a child.

Dr. George Tichenor had ties to Liberty. A Civil War-era

doctor, he's been called by some the South's greatest surgeon. He developed Dr. Tichenor's Antiseptic, still sold out of New Orleans. A person with multiple interests, he's called the father of the Mississippi River levee system for his efforts to prevent flooding.

Before becoming a surgeon, Tichenor was a Sergeant in the Confederate Calvary. While serving in the army, he moonlighted in the study of medicine. How did he find the time?

Jerry Clower, country comedian called The Mouth of the South, grew up in Liberty and Amite County. He was a Grand Ole Opry star, probably the best known fertilizer salesman ever. My folks told me they grew up with the people Jerry told stories about. I remember his sister being at my dad's funeral.

Liberty was among the first towns in the United States to erect a monument to Confederate war dead. About 1,000 of the county's men went off to fight, 279 of them didn't come back. The dead are memorialized on the monument. On my recent visit, I noted that nine of those 279 were Anders. Wish I knew more about my family history.

Liberty is the county seat of Amite County. The courthouse is the oldest in Mississippi still in use. I know the courthouse also has the best and longest sidewalk in town. As a kid I made hundreds of trips, if not a couple of thousand, around it on a scooter, a prehistoric version of a two-wheeled skateboard with a steering wheel added.

There's a US veteran's memorial on the courthouse lawn, put

there about 10 years ago. All county veterans were invited to write a letter to enclose in a time capsule to be opened in about 40 more years. I did. Perhaps my kids or grandkids will be interested in what I had to say, hope so.

*Amite County courthouse and veterans memorial.*

Across the street from the courthouse is the office of the Southern Herald, our weekly newspaper now for more than 140 years. It's the oldest business in the county. I still subscribe, still recognize family names from way back when.

I visited Liberty on a clear sunny day, but as usual it was about to flood. A flood of memories. Born in 1943 in Dr. Butler's clinic in Liberty, next to the Liberty Barber Shop, I lived there through 1955 and the 6th grade. Returned briefly in 1957. Riding around town, I saw the houses we lived in. Thought about my first

Christmases. Saw the hill I learned to ride a bike on. Noticed the foundation where my dad's welding shop stood.

Went by the drive-in from which we launched watermelon raids. The carnival grounds where we saw: "The Horse With His Tail Where His Head Ought To Be." For a quarter, you saw that his tail was tied over the feed trough, but you had to keep the secret. The ice plant my dad owned, with the fresh fish room, hundreds of live frogs. Whole lotta croaking going on.

Remembered Patsy, my neighbor and classmate, playing cops and robbers with me, long before I thought of being either one. Thought of the open septic ditches, where wild onions grew. Don't eat onions to this day. Drove by my old elementary school, now a grocery store. In 1st grade I sat about where the bananas are now, so if you've ever thought of me as a banana-brain, you weren't far from the truth.

Just too many memories to detail them all.

If you've ever flown on an airliner, you've probably been close to a product made in Liberty, but I hope you didn't get to use it. Aircruisers Inc., a division of the Zodiac Company of France, manufactures such products for big planes as evacuation chutes and life vests.

So this is Liberty, Mississippi, my hometown. We celebrated our Bi-Centennial in 2009. I also remember the 150 year celebration, 50 years before that. My dad grew a beard, the only time I ever saw him with one. If you showed up without a beard back then, you wound up in jail. Just a part of our good old fashioned Southern hospitality, I suppose. Actually it was all in good clean fun!

The Good Lord was willing and Tan Yard Creek didn't rise so I was there enjoying the 200th year of the place that always has been - and always will be - home. Why not visit your hometown soon?

Someone once even said: "You're never homeless so long as you're sleeping on the streets of your hometown."

## GROWING UP, SHRINKING DOWN

As we grow older, everything shrinks, doesn't it? The houses that seemed huge when we were little don't look that way when we become adults, and our hometowns also seem much smaller.

Growing up in Amite County, our towns of under a thousand people seemed big enough to me. Monthly shopping took us to McComb. Getting new school clothes each year from Sears Roebuck or Penney's required a visit to Jackson or Baton Rouge. My dad would take me with him on work trips to places like Crosby or Natchez.

But the ultimate for shopping and fun was going to New Orleans. Canal Street, Pontchartrain Beach, Mardi Gras parades.

All those cities and towns were my universe in the late 1940s and 1950s. It seemed a massive area.

The 1970s found me on an Air Force plane, returning from Washington, D. C., to San Antonio, Texas. We'd landed at Memphis to refuel. There was a Federal airway over Mississippi, like a highway in the sky, and we were headed west on it at about 10,000 feet altitude.

Our twin engine aircraft had no extra oxygen supply, so we flew relatively low. It was dark, and Highway 24 was on our right side. The navigator tapped me on the shoulder when Liberty appeared below us.

Looking out a small right side window, just a single small line of street lights – Main Street - could be seen. Gloster was just ahead, and slightly to the northwest was Natchez. Vicksburg and Jackson were illuminated to the north. McComb was still visible behind us.

On the left side, Centreville was almost directly underneath. Baton Rouge was brightly lit and the nighttime glow of New Orleans was just over the horizon. My whole childhood world was contained out there in two small oval windows.

That world had truly shrunk. But my point of view had greatly enlarged. Still, Amite County was at the center of things, no matter how big or small, and to this day I've either been coming from it with plans to return, or headed that direction.

## Chapter 2

RAILROADING OUR THOUGHTS

**LOVIN' THE COLOR**

RECENTLY WE TALKED about how the world shrinks as we get older. The world loses clarity and color, too. As a youngster in Amite County, the pine trees were very green, year round. Percy Quinn State Park or Amite River water at the swimming hole out by Peoria, or at Bates Bridge, had a startling clarity, sometimes a bright blue color.

The apples from the grocery store on Main Street in Liberty on the way to school were a delicious red, if "delicious" may be used to describe a tint. Rubbing them on my blue jeans, of course, was – and still is – the accepted way of making 'em really shine! Almost hated to eat them. Well, almost.

Living on county dirt roads, one got used to that dusty covering that most everything had, especially if you lived close to the traffic. But the dust, to my young eyes, was a clearly defined light brown. Almost a clean looking dust.

Returning to Amite County across the years, it seemed the color of things got less spectacular as time went on. The brights weren't as bright and the colors weren't as vivid. Was my enthusiasm slipping, or what?

During the last 12 months, you really looked hazy. But guess what? There was another, more logical reason. My eyeglass prescription was changed three times. If you're older, you understand. Cataracts!

Mine were growing like well-tended baby carrots in a hungry rabbit's garden. Sorry, younger folks, cataracts are inevitable, according to what the eye doc tells me. So, get ready!

During the past two weeks, my peepers have been overhauled, one per week. Next time you're in my line of vision, Amite County, you're gonna look great! And you looked pretty good before. So if you catch me staring at you, it's just that I didn't really see you during previous visits.

Those pine trees and even the dirt roads will both be very colorful again, and back to 20-20! Thank you, Lord, for the blessings of modern medicine.

Hey, there's already a Gloster trip planned in my immediate future. I'm going by the Grocery Store to get me an apple!

## IT'S A SMALL WORLD!

Those of us who leave our town, our area, our state…when young…are in for serious changes when we return.

The only thing that stays the same in life is change. It's always happening.

But remnants of what we remember are usually in place. The basic qualities of a hometown - a home county - a state – remain the same. And since it's "our" place, we're quick to defend it, especially if others point out to us what they think are its shortcomings.

My family left Amite County in 1955 for Oregon when Mr. Alvin Sansing of Gloster took his sawmill there. My dad went with him as the millwright. Mr. Chuck Sansing, who now operates the Grocery Store in Gloster, is remembered by me as a four year old in Ashland, Oregon. I was the yard boy who cut Mr. Alvin Sansing's grass with a sling blade, who did odd jobs around the sawmill. Sweeping up on weekends, getting things ready for the coming Monday morning.

Isn't it a small world we live in!

## VISITING PERCY QUINN AGAIN

Growing up in Mississippi, we didn't have many Big Boy Toys around our house because finances usually didn't allow them, but sometimes my father had a speedboat. If so, it was an inboard-powered Chris Craft. He had no patience for outboard motors.

A favorite place to take our boat was Percy Quin State Park, near McComb. I recall being there at only five years of age.

Recently, I've revisited Percy Quin. It's a beautiful place that's only gotten better. The Civilian Construction Corps developed it in the 1930s. The park is about 1700 acres, and has RV sites - group camping – lakefront cabins – a lodge - Convention Center – tennis courts – archery range – and hiking trails.

Of course there's fishing and boating in 700 acre Lake Tangipahoa. Researching this article is the first time I've known the lake by that name. We just always called it Percy Quin Lake. Mr. Quin was a U. S. representative from Mississippi in the 1920s.

A public 18 hole golf course, Quail Hollow, is also nearby. This state park is often rated #1 in Mississippi by visitors! This and other beautiful lakes and rivers are some of the reasons we have to see our area as a glass half full, not half empty.

On the day of my visit, 13 year old Walker Brignac of Mandeville, Louisiana, was at Percy Quin with his grandfather, A. J. Brignac Jr., of Loranger, Louisiana, trying to catch the big one. It was on a lazy Sunday afternoon. Mr. Brignac had retired from his job the previous Friday, and hadn't wasted any time in getting his grandson outdoors for the weekend.

Percy Quin State Park is less than 30 miles from Gloster. Get over and enjoy it yourself sometime. Take your child or your grandchild fishing there, as our visitor from Louisiana did!

*Young Walker Brignac of Louisiana at Percy Quin State Park.*

## THE PERPETUAL SEARCH
## FOR PERPETUAL MOTION

My father, George Davis Anders, built a portable sawmill in Amite County during 1949 and obtained a U. S. Patent for it. About a dozen were eventually manufactured. Here's a photo I had hidden away. One still exists near Liberty on the property of Mr. Tate McGehee who has been kind enough to let my sister and me look at it. Mr. McGehee and his father used it to make a living in years past.

*My father standing, right, on his portable sawmill, 1949,
Anders Machine Shop, Liberty.*

*What's left of the McGehee sawmill after almost 70 years.*

Yesterday my wife and I purchased a pallet of sod to fill in some blank spots of grass in our yard. I remembered back when my dad built a house near Liberty and needed sod. He refused to pay the price - or maybe we didn't have the money - so he quickly built his own "sod cutter". It had a blade that ran horizontally about three inches deep. We headed for the pasture on the Gillsburg Road at my grandfather's place where there was some pretty grass, pulling the apparatus behind the bulldozer, and soon we had plenty of sod.

My father had a mind for invention or creative building. About the ultimate pursuit of engineering is the concept of perpetual motion. That is, an energy producing device like a motor that will run perpetually and drive something, without using a fuel source. You can imagine how popular that would be with gasoline companies. My dad was always thinking on that topic.

During the latter part of his life, he produced a model made of wood, a device that looked somewhat like a circular saw blade, with very large teeth, maybe a dozen. Each "tooth" surface had a gradually rising portion, then another portion that dropped off suddenly, but not quite straight down. There were spring-loaded rollers that gradually went up each portion of the gradual rise, then dropped off - at different times - suddenly, propelled strongly downward by the spring. The sudden downward push produced energy and propelled the device, as other spring-loaded rollers gradually advanced up their "teeth".

You could spin that contraption, it would start running, and would continue for several minutes - clack! - clack! - clack! -clack! - clack! - clack! - making lots of racket. It wasn't machined in a precision way so friction or drag, enemies of perpetual motion, slowly won out, and the "motor" would eventually stop. But my dad kept working on it. I was amazed that he came up with it in the first place.

If you can't picture the device, don't worry, that's not the important part. My father passed away in 1982 and his perpetual motion device mysteriously disappeared. Wish I had it but it's gone. Some years later, I was reading an autobiography of Charles Lindbergh, the first person to fly solo across the Atlantic Ocean. Lindbergh's father was apparently like mine, a creative kind of person who made things. In his book, Lindbergh described a device his father had made that sounded just like the machine my dad built. I was startled!!

Did my father and Lindbergh's father have the same idea independently? Lindbergh's father died in 1924, my dad was just eight then. My father wasn't much of a reader, although he would study technical information he was interested in. Had my dad run across something of the senior Mr. Lindbergh's thoughts on perpetual motion? Had he seen a photo of Lindbergh's design? Or was it all coincidence?

Those questions are one of life's little mysteries about my father that I'll never solve. The sort of thing that makes you wish you'd sought more information from someone when they were still around.

# THE TRAIN THAT SAVED THE SPACE SHUTTLE

Back Home, I find that our area has an abundance of folks who've led interesting and productive lives. We can all learn from your achievements, but we need your help. Call the Wilk-Amite Record and tell us what you've done and we'll turn it into a story that everyone can enjoy!

Mr. David Hoffman of Woodville MS is retired from NASA. His wife, Dorothea, is a Crosby native and is writing a monthly column for the Wilk-Amite Record, called Here, There, and Everywhere. We know you'll like it! Mr. Hoffman was in charge of the ground transportation system, the "train", at Cape Canaveral that carried the space shuttle from its hangar to the launching pad.

In 1982, the shuttle was forced by weather conditions to land in New Mexico at an alternate runway. Making that last minute change was a challenge, as you'll read in a story that David Hoffman has written for us, but NASA - and David - made it work. For 15 years, I lived very near where that landing took place, although it was later than 1982 when I was there.

The shuttle landed in New Mexico just that once. The gypsum at the White Sands runway - it's actually not sand but gypsum - embedded itself into the shuttle's surface and was very difficult and costly to remove. But the people I know who saw the landing still talk about it. I think NASA would have used White Sands only in a dire emergency after that because of the problems with the gypsum.

At the time, my family and I lived in San Antonio, TX. The shuttle, carried atop a giant Boeing 747 aircraft, routinely landed there at Kelly AFB for refueling en route from Edwards AFB, CA, back to Florida. In the photo shown, taken probably in 1979, I'd taken the two boys I had then to Kelly to see it. They're Bryan, second from left, and Brett, on the far right. They were 11 and 12, respectively.

*Bryan and Brett with friends, 1979, Kelly AFB, Texas.*

Partly inspired by what they saw, Brett later flew Navy F-18 fighters and then the same type of huge 747 aircraft for Cathay Pacific Airlines, a British-owned company. Bryan, born deaf, couldn't fly but became a software engineer for a company that works for NASA.

Just a couple of days ago, Bryan e-mailed me a photo of the shuttle Discovery atop a 747, along with a NASA T-38 jet, as they arrived in Washington, DC. Discovery will be permanently displayed at the Smithsonian Museum. Bryan and a friend watched the arrival. His friend took the photograph. On closer examination of our picture of 32 years ago, and this 2012 one, the tail number of the Boeing 747 is the same! It's the same airplane. My son didn't know at the time he was looking at the identical aircraft he was pictured in front of when he was a little boy.

NASA had purchased it from American Airlines, and in the 1979 photo it still had American Airlines striping. It's since been repainted, but at least we can say there's one government agency that gets some life out of something they own! NASA had two of these big 747s, #905 and #911, but #911 was retired in February of this year.

I just hope they remembered to change the oil between flights. It's been used a long time. We hope you enjoy Mr. Hoffman's story about the train that saved the space shuttle!

**GETTING RAILROADED**

Amite County has a rich if diluted history in railroading. We haven't captured much physical evidence of that history, at least in a place such as a museum.

There was the Liberty-White Railroad, a combination of a narrow gauge logging railway and a standard gauge passenger line from McComb to Liberty. Small segments of the old rail bed still exist, if you know where to look. In Peoria, on private

18

property, a little depot building still stands. The Liberty-White Railroad ran from 1902 until 1921.

There was the Gloster Southern Railroad, a freight line running from Gloster to Slaughter, Louisiana, to transport Georgia-Pacific products. It started in 1990 and effectively ceased operation in 2002.

*Gloster Southern boxcar displayed in Gloster, Mississippi, 2012.*

The Yazoo-Mississippi Valley Railroad hauled passengers to Camp Van Dorn in Centreville during WWII. Many of those riders, of course, were military men.

If we don't make a strong written record and accomplish a collection of railroad artifacts, the information and the physical remains eventually disappear for future generations.

Living out West for several years, my wife and I became interested in the Cumbres & Toltec Scenic Railroad which still runs over 64 miles from Chama, New Mexico, to Antonito, Colorado. It was built in 1880, an engineering feat. It's America's most authentic steam-powered railroad, and received National Historical Designation earlier this year. Portions of the route climb to over 10,000 feet. We joined its Friends Support Committee a few years ago and are currently working a two-week volunteer stint.

This summer, there are seven one-week work sessions. A variety of people from over the United States come to help, at no pay. Some repair old railcars, some paint those already restored. Some home states I've noted are Colorado and New Mexico, of course, but also California, Missouri, Alabama, Florida, Arizona, Mississippi and New York. About 50 persons are here for each of the week long sessions we're attending.

My wife is working in food preparation. I'm acting as a chronicler, documenting the progress of projects through written accounts and photographs.

In years past, the Cumbres & Toltec was a part of the Denver & Rio Grande Railroad which ran from Denver, Colorado, to Santa Fe, New Mexico. It supported various mining operations, logging, and oil drilling activities.

Since 1970, it's been a historical narrow gauge railroad for passenger traffic, a joint project of the states of Colorado and New Mexico. A commission of persons from both states administers its affairs.

Chama, New Mexico, where we're staying, is a beautiful place in the mountains, with the small city's elevation at more than 7,000 feet. I love Mississippi but one benefit of being here is dodging a small portion of our Southern summertime. Temperatures here are only in the 80s during daytime, and down into the 40s at night. Believe it or not, a heater and a blanket felt good!

*Cumbres & Toltec arrives at Chama, New Mexico, during 2013.*

What we're doing won't change the world, of course, but it is fun to have a small part in helping preserve this little slice of history. The real heroes are the hard workers who toiled years ago to build a railroad in places you can't believe until you look over the edge of a cliff several hundred feet high, way up in the Rocky Mountains.

When old #489 comes chugging into Chama daily at 4 pm from Antonito, with happy folks aboard including many children, it's a beautiful sight! We thank the Good Lord for the strength and opportunity to do this.

Author's note, added June 2017: The Cumbres & Toltec Scenic Steam Railroad was voted the best train ride in North America during 2016 in a USA Today poll. It's a definite bucket list item. I trained, tested and qualified as a docent – a historical guide – last year and would welcome your visit. Would love to conduct your on-board tour! Some of you may know Billy and Arlene Crider of next door Pike County. Billy has worked as a docent for many years with the Cumbres & Toltec.

*Billy and Arlene Crider of Pike County, Mississippi.*
*She is a native of Amite County.*

*Chapter 3*

GOOD PEOPLE
AND GOOD FRIENDS

**HAPPY NEW YEAR!**
**LOOKING BACK TO LOOK AT THE FUTURE**

SOMETIMES, GREETING A New Year, it's good to look at historical events that ultimately guaranteed a good future for Americans. In December's paper, I mentioned my good fortune in being able to visit Hawaii during the Christmas holidays. Luckily, my time there coincided with the 71st anniversary of the attack on Pearl Harbor, and I couldn't resist the opportunity to attend the ceremony.

As expected, high ranking officials presided and they said the right things. Hawaiian trade winds blew briskly and U. S. flags popped and snapped, looking great. It was good to see but I knew that survivors of the attack would be in attendance. About 30 were. Thus my real goal was to meet some of them, shake their hands, and tell them "thank you" on behalf of you, our Wilk-Amite Record readers. I wanted to ask what they remember most about that fateful day.

Mr. Robert P. Irwin of Cameron Park, California, and Mr. Ewalt Schatz of Moreno Valley, California, were both 18 year old Navy men who survived the attack, on separate ships. They've known each other in later years from having been neighbors in Cameron Park where Mr. Schatz also formerly lived, and were sitting together this year. I'll save you the math, and mention that each is now 89. They graciously allowed me to join them after the speeches.

According to Wikipedia, the battleship USS Pennsylvania was in dry dock in the Pearl Harbor navy yard when the attack began. She was one of the first ships to open fire as enemy dive and torpedo bombers roared out of the high overcast. Japanese aircraft did not succeed in repeated attempts to torpedo the dry dock, but *Pennsylvania* and the surrounding dock areas were severely strafed. The crew of one 5 inch gun mount was wiped out when a bomb struck the starboard side of her boat deck and exploded.

Destroyers Cassin and Downes, just forward of *Pennsylvania* in the dry dock, were seriously damaged by bomb hits. *Pennsylvania* was pockmarked by flying fragments. A part of a torpedo tube from *Downes*, about 1,000 lb in weight, was blown onto the forecastle of *Pennsylvania*. She had 15 men killed (including her executive officer), 14 missing in action, and 38 wounded.

Mr. Irwin was assigned to the USS Pennsylvania. When the attack began, his first thought was that it was an exercise, but that notion was quickly dispelled. He was at an island barracks since the ship was in dry dock, and hopped onto a truck for a quick ride to the harbor. Bob Irwin responded to a call for volunteers to bring up ammunition from below decks for a 5 inch gun used as an anti-aircraft weapon.

Before Mr. Irwin went below, he saw three bombs fall from a Japanese plane onto the USS Arizona, and watched as one of those bombs penetrated the Arizona's deck, striking the magazine. He witnessed the complete destruction of the Arizona that resulted in more than 1,100 of her crewmembers being killed. The catastrophic explosion is his lasting, most vivid memory. Among the killed, missing and wounded on his own ship, the Pennsylvania, were many of his friends.

The USS Patterson was a destroyer moored at Pearl Harbor when the Japanese carrier-based planes swooped in. Her gunners sped to battle stations, opened fire, and blasted one enemy plane out of the sky. Within an hour the destroyermen were searching for possible enemy submarines off the harbor entrance.

Following the attack, *Patterson* patrolled the Hawaiian Sea Frontier in the screen of aircraft carrier Saratoga without finding trace of the enemy. On 28 December, returning from patrol, she rescued 19 survivors of merchant ship *Marimi* adrift for several days after having been torpedoed by a Japanese submarine.

Mr. Schatz was a Patterson crewmember. He'd never been allowed to actually fire the .50 caliber machine gun he volunteered to man during the attack. Previously, the only persons who'd operated it were experienced hands so that better scores were achieved by the ship during graded drills. Those older hands, though, were caught up in the repair of a boiler. The sight of buildings exploding on nearby Ford Island immediately convinced him the event was the real thing. Quickly, he found the machine gun was easy to aim since every fifth round was a "tracer" which had a definite color he could see.

What he remembers best? Ewalt Schatz said a Japanese plane passed overhead so close that he looked right into the pilot's face and saw him so well, he thought he might recognize him if he ever met him on the street, or from pictures, in later years. Try as he might, though, he never has. Mr. Schatz believed then the pilot was looking directly at him, although across time he concluded the pilot was more likely intensely studying the ship as a target.

Mr. Schatz was credited as the USS Patterson gunner who shot a Japanese plane out of the sky. It was a different plane from the one in which he looked so closely into the pilot's face.

The two gentlemen were gracious, humble, and retain a great sense of humor. Mr. Irwin still flies his own small plane, an Aeronca. Mr. Schatz, in reference to his having shot down a plane, remarked: "Heck, it may be true or not. A lot of our people were shooting at those planes besides me." I gave up my seat between them to an Australian lady, and they were happy to welcome her in my place. True Navy men, both still like the pretty girls!

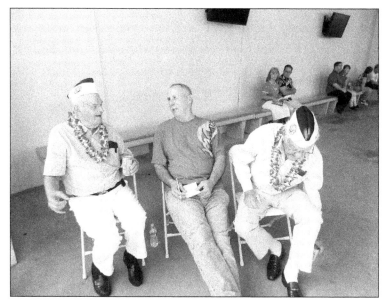

*Robert Irwin (l) and Ewalt Schatz (r) with the author,*
*Pearl Harbor, Hawaii, 2012.*

It was a privilege on December 7, 2012, to represent you, the good people of Amite County, Mississippi, in thanking these men for their courageous actions on December 7, 1941. They struck me as regular good citizens, patriotic, who acted with bravery under fire, caught up in an extraordinary event they still remember well.

May God bless them, and all of you, in this New Year of 2013!

## REMEMBERING THE
## HARD-HEADED DUTCHMAN

Happy New Year! Resolutions are in order. Pardon me if I look backwards at the last day of 2012 in forming mine.

Leaving Mississippi in 1955, I lived in several places during my work career. There are good people everywhere, and some became lifelong friends. In 1970, I answered a newspaper ad to meet with some folks forming the San Antonio (Texas) Canoe Club.

The leader was a San Antonio fireman, Leslie Teague, Jr. We were the same age. After that, we partnered up as a canoe racing team. We camped and paddled many rivers across the United States. In 1987, our attempt to break the Guinness Book of World Records for paddling the length of the Mississippi River - 2,510 miles - was unsuccessful, but the try was worthwhile. We began at Lake Itasca, Minnesota, where the river forms, where it's small enough to practically step across.

We logged trips on the Lower Canyons of the Rio Grande, adjoining Mexico; and on most rivers in Texas, including paddling the Texas Water Safari in what's called the world's toughest boat race, 260 non-stop miles on the San Marcos and Guadalupe Rivers. Our best time, moving 24/7, was 55 hours. Upside down one time in tornado-like conditions in the Gulf of Mexico, off the coast near Seadrift, Texas, holding onto our boat, we finally got to shore.

In late 1986 we'd launched from Natchez where the Isle of Capri casino boat now is moored and paddled to St. Francisville,

Louisiana. The Mississippi was just four inches from overflowing its banks, something that didn't faze my friend. My ole pard described himself as a Hard-Headed Dutchman, and if you weren't doing your best during daytime, you were Burning Daylight. To him, not a good thing!

*Les Teague at St.Francisville, Louisiana,*
*rainy day on the Mississippi River, 1986.*

Short story: we stepped on a lot of snakes together. He became and remained an absolute best friend, my standard-bearer for the concept of friendship. Our families lived within three miles, and if a barn needed building or an emergency came along, he was there.

This past December 18th, I made a quick dash to Texas, his wife having informed me of his deteriorating condition. He was in hospice care, the terminal effects of Lou Gehrig's disease. He was ready to meet his Lord, but I encouraged him to make it through Christmas for his family's sake. Amazingly, he did. On December 31st, though, having just left Gloster, I received a call from his oldest son.

Les III is a Lt Colonel who works for the U. S. Army Corps of Engineers at Vicksburg. "Dad died just 45 minutes ago," he said, great emotion in his voice. Les III may be a colonel but he's better known to me as French Fry, since he ate a lot of mine when he was little. It's one of the saddest calls I've ever gotten.

For 2013, I resolve to try to be the kind of friend to others his father was to me. May he rest in peace. May your New Year be filled with people of his caliber, and may you not Burn Daylight.

## A WRITING PLACE

Last week I lamented the loss of a best friend. Any of us with best friends knows we can count the number of true ones on the fingers of one hand.

I've got some spare fingers. It's occurred to me…what am I doing to assign new people or those I knew formerly to those finger spaces? The answer, sadly, is: not much.

To honor my best friend in Texas, Les, who just passed away, I'm putting together a photographic memory of our adventures together for his wife and children. He and I canoed all over the U. S. but his family tells me there are no pictures, of him doing that, just of other people. He was that kind of person, not self-centered.

So I've been digging in some dusty places, saying hello to some spiders, and I've come up with photos. I've also come up with some pictures of folks I was friends with a long time ago, and have lost track of. Twelve years ago, in 2001, I visited with one of them in Wenatchee, Washington,  His wife, Cheryl, died of breast cancer in Texas way before that so he sold his house, bought 30 acres on the Wenatchee River, and moved West to start a new life called Wenatchee Water Sports.

My grandmother, Carrie Rice, who's buried in Liberty Cemetery, was formerly a Walker of Pike County. My Maw Maw Rice knew everyone in the family. When you needed information, she was the go-to person. How did she do it?

My aunt reminds me that my grandmother had a "writing place" and sat at it almost daily, writing a letter to someone. And when you write someone, they often write back.

So this week I'm taking a page out of Maw Maw Rice's book and writing some old friends, since I have space on my hands to make good use of some vacant fingers where I can name some new best friends. I don't want to be without best friends, but have come to the realization it's up to me to do something about it.

This morning, I wrote Morey a letter. Let's see what happens. Oh, if Casey Campbell has room on the back page, I'll include one of those dusty photos I found, of Les, who died December 31st.

## YANKEE BOB, A GOOD MAN

Wish me luck the next couple of weeks. I'm headed to the Land of the Yankee. Annually, I take a trip to near Cooperstown in New York State, and it's that time.

Cooperstown is the home of the Baseball Hall of Fame, and I visit it every other year. As a boy growing up in Amite County, my baseball hero was Mickey Mantle. He was a country boy from Oklahoma and seemed much like us in manner.

A friend of mine met Mickey once in Okinawa as Mantle toured military bases. My friend said he was the nicest man, very down home, easy to talk to. At the Baseball Hall of Fame, he's not the most popular player represented, and the display about him doesn't feature much more than his game jersey. I asked why.

A staff person told me that Mickey was disappointed that Babe Ruth's area was so much bigger, and complained about it, and as is the nature of things, his own display was kept to a minimum. To me it seems that Babe Ruth was the signature player in baseball. But I still like Mickey Mantle and remember watching him on television in my early years when I lived in Liberty.

Each year I pick out another attraction that's reasonably close and go see it. Those have included Niagara Falls, the U. S. Military Academy at West Point, Howe's Cavern near Albany, Lake George in the Adirondacks, etc.

I wrote here about such a side trip I made to Maine to find people who knew O. C. McDavid who owned the Wilk-Amite Record in the late 1940s. He summered in Winter Harbor, Maine, and was very well-known and popular. His son owned our newspaper for 10 years during the 1950s, and moved on to become editor of the Houston Chronicle.

Going north, I'll see my middle son and his family who live in Virginia, and an old friend who lives in Maryland. Coming south I'll leave the usual route for my side trip. I'll visit Lancaster, Pennsylvania, then drive to Dover, Delaware. I've never been to the state of Delaware and look forward to that. Continuing south, I'll cross Chesapeake Bay on a 17 mile bridge back into Virginia where I'll visit old friends who live in Virginia Beach.

Why do I go to New York? Several years ago, when I was in law enforcement, my partner and I were ambushed and he was killed. He was a native of New York State. I promised his mother and two brothers that I would visit them annually and they've welcomed me into their family. We reflect on the happy times that we shared, though they were at different phases of his life, with my friend, their son and brother.

Deputy Sheriff Robert Hedman, Jr., was just 53 years old. He was a good man. He was one of my three best friends. He was courageous. A three-year old girl was being held hostage, and he gave his life trying to save her. In some crazy way, it worked and she lived. He died doing a job he loved. He had a grandson her age, and he wasn't just a deputy sheriff doing his job. He was Grandpa Bob as well.

*Deputy Sheriff Bob Hedman, Jr., 2004.*

If you've got a spare prayer laying around, say one for Bob's mother. She's 80 now, has successfully fought breast cancer over the last year, and has dealt with the tragic death of her son with grace. She and her other two sons might be Yankees, but they're my Yankees and I love them.

*Chapter 4*

# Cemeteries, the River and the Ocean

## AMITE COUNTY CEMETERIES

As this is written, it's Mother's Day, and it's hard to believe that it will soon be five years since I last held my mother's hand. She passed away on July 11, 2008, and I miss her.

Last Sunday, back home in Amite County for Liberty's Heritage Days, I stood at her grave for a few minutes and reflected on the good times we had. The day before, I'd visited the gravesite of a distant relative, R. W. Anders, a Confederate veteran, who'd died in 1906. His burial place is in a remote location in the Homochitto National Forest.

*R.W. Anders, 1843 – 1906, grave in remote site
in Homochitto National Forest.*

My mother, my father and other family members are interred at Robinson Baptist Church cemetery in the Peoria community, "out towards McComb" as many of us in our county would say. Those two short trips caused me to think of some unsung heroes in our midst.

Policemen? Firemen? Well, most of those are certainly unsung heroes, but I thought of a more unlikely category. Those who maintain cemeteries.

Across my conscious lifetime, perhaps 65 of the 70 years I've been around and might have noticed such things, I've never visited the cemetery in Peoria next to the little church when it hasn't been immaculate. Spring, summer, fall, or winter, the grass is mowed...the limbs and leaves are cleaned up...the fence is repaired, the gates are unlocked but closed.

As one like you, who's mowed and trimmed a yard across perhaps 55 of my 70 years, just stop and think of how much work that represents. Sure, through the cemetery association, I've paid a small fee for "perpetual care", but certainly it hasn't been way enough. Multiply the work it takes to cut your own yard by an acre or two or more and toss in hundreds, perhaps a few thousand headstones, all of which have four sides and are raised off the ground and the trimming that goes with that, and you begin to appreciate the effort it takes to maintain a cemetery.

Yes, the little one-burial site hidden in the Homochitto has fallen into disrepair, but the tattered remains of a little Confederate flag were draped on what's left of the fence. Folks, that small flag didn't fall out of the sky and land there. Some good soul trooped out into the deep, dark woods years ago and left it.

To those who do such things, be they city workers or private cemetery association workers or just fine people, thank you. May your labors be considered a good work as described in the Bible and may God bless you. When I visit the Peoria cemetery, the obvious dedication of those who've kept it looking so good always makes me stop and think on the last verse of "Amazing Grace".

"When we've been there 10,000 years, bright shining as the sun, we've no less days to sing God's praise, than when we first begun." Okay, 10,000 years from now, our earthly burial places will likely be gone, but it won't be for lack of effort on the part of those who take care of them now. You are appreciated!

*Robinson Baptist Church cemetery - Peoria, Mississippi.*

## THE CONFEDERATE CEMETERY
## AT CLINTON, LOUISIANA

Our nearby Louisiana neighbor, Clinton, has something in common with Liberty. The Amite County courthouse is the oldest in Mississippi. The East Feliciana courthouse in Clinton, dating from 1840, is the oldest in Louisiana.

Clinton's Confederate Cemetery, a couple of blocks south of the courthouse, is a fascinating place. Here's a walking tour description of this hallowed burial ground.

"This historic cemetery is where many prominent Clintonians are buried including Susan Bostwick and James Holmes who were developers of the town. Also buried here is John Rhea who was a founder of the Clinton and Port Hudson Railroad and president of the West Florida Convention which established an independent nation in the Florida Parishes in 1810. A walk through this cemetery is a walk through the history of Clinton, war, yellow fever epidemics, the Civil War and early hard times. The unmarked graves of Civil War soldiers are on the Western edge of the burial ground."

I was in Clinton recently and had an hour to spend before a business appointment, so I took time to walk through the cemetery. It was my second visit, and the last was more hurried. I was interested in looking at Civil War grave sites.

It's my understanding that as many as 600 Confederate soldiers may lie there in unmarked graves. Wounded in nearby fighting, they supposedly were buried in trenches.

The day of my visit was a beautiful day, and a cemetery can be one of the most relaxing places to spend time, just wander around. While I took it easy, two men working on the open grassy area of the fenced grounds caught my attention. They had a metal detector and were using little orange marker flags in a systematic search. I drifted their direction.

I introduced myself to Bill Rome and Larry Gates who both live in the area. They were finding and removing heavy nails from the ground and marking those locations with the flags. They explained that small markers had been placed at 248 places where graves of Confederates had been identified by a friend who had a ground radar unit. But he passed away before the data could be codified. Groundskeepers had then removed the markers in order to maintain the grounds, but had replaced them with the nails.

One step forward, two steps backward. There was no harmful intent, though, and admittedly a cemetery with tombstones and other markers has to be one of the most difficult pieces of this good earth to mow properly.

Bill Rome and Larry Gates were doing their best to save the results of their friend's good work. Bill is a Baton Rouge High School and LSU grad, but Larry was the one wearing a LSU t-shirt. Oddly, he attended the University of South Carolina, but a Gamecock who's working in a Confederate cemetery in Clinton, Louisiana, while wearing such clothing can be forgiven for such a small indiscretion!

Bill and I shared some pleasant memories of my former mother-in-law who was his calculus teacher at BRHS in 1966. "Tough but good," he remembered her from school, which is about the same remembrance I have of her when as an Istrouma High School student, I crossed town and dated her daughter.

Thanks, Bill and Larry, for your great efforts, and for remembering and honoring those soldiers who were doing their duty, as they saw it, for God and country. You are appreciated.


**JUS' SAYIN'**

Gloster, home of the apostrophe. Maybe the town's spellin' should now be Gloster'.

It's springtime and flowers are bloomin' and grass is growin'. But that's not all.

Do you live elsewhere and haven't been to Gloster in two or three years? You're missin' out.

The DRAX plant is comin' along. Construction crews are buildin' and concretin', making serious progress. Landlords are rentin'. Tenants are lookin' for a place to stay.

Highway 24 in the mornin' between 7 and 9 should be labeled the Gloster 500. Delivery trucks are racin' and log trucks are loggin' and oil tankers are rollin'.

DOT is checkin' and watchin'. Restaurant owners are cookin' and servin'. Places like La Cabana, Café 24, and the Gloster Café are doing well. One recent early evening, I counted 12 vehicles, mostly work trucks, at La Cabana, a line of six persons waitin'.

No crayfish in its right mind would crawl into town any day near Thursday, lest it wind up in the pot at the Gloster Café. Thursday nights there are hummin', as are all other weekdays.

Sure, it's raining some, and some workers are muddin', but that's okay. The same boots that brought wet dirt onto the Café 24 floor recently had wallets just above them that left some green stuff. And that's encouragin'!

Stores like Betty's Attic, Dollar General, Family Dollar, and Spillman's are stockin' and sellin'.

RV Parks, by the way, are overflowin', and that means some-thing good.

Sometimes when things are down we tell ourselves that "bet-ter days are ahead". In Gloster, they're here now as things are progressin'.

Don't miss out. If you have an idea or are thinkin' of starting a business, now is the time to be joinin' in. There's a nice window waitin' to be opened at this time, a window of opportunity.

Maybe – just maybe – some of this is happenin' because folks in Gloster and other nearby places are in church, prayin'. Let's hope so.


## A RIVER RUNS THROUGH IT

The Amite River is an ever-present part of our life in Amite County. Indeed, the county is named for the river. Near Gloster we cross the west fork; just above Peoria on Highway 24 and near Gillsburg we see the east fork.

Many who grew up in Amite County learned how to swim in the Amite River, thus it holds many memories. I am one of those. On Sunday afternoons, my family would picnic near Peoria.

The east fork begins in Lincoln County, while the west fork begins in Franklin County. The two branches join forces very near the Mississippi/Louisiana state line. Altogether it flows

117 miles until it empties into Lake Maurepas, which itself empties into Lake Pontchartrain. Across the years, due to widening and straightening, the length has decreased by six miles.

The lower 37 miles or so are navigable by boat. In the late 1800s, large steamboats plied that section, transporting people and crops like cotton. Once there were many sawmills lining the banks there, since logs could be floated to the mills.

The Indians, whose name for the river meant "friendship", also lived along the river until the early 1800s. It is believed it was named in 1699. The Indians made arrowheads from rocks along the river, a commodity which they traded with other Indian nations.

Now the Louisiana section especially has many hunting and fishing camps. Canals have been dug in many places to the river. The water in the canals becomes stagnant in low water, promoting the growth of undesirable plant life. For many, though, it is a vacation paradise. Only about 5% of the shoreline has been developed in this manner.

You can canoe the upper forks but be prepared to get in and out of the boat often as you cross logs. If you try boating it, just go a short distance on the first trip, from one bridge to the next, since it may take you much longer than you might believe ahead of time. If there is a road alongside, the river's length next to it may be two to three times the distance of the road.

Of course you wouldn't do this without knowing that many water moccasins would be enjoying the river right along beside you! During 2012 and 2013, three adult Asian carp were identified in the lower Amite River by the Louisiana Wildlife & Fisheries Department. They were believed to have come in through the Bonne Carre Spillway during a 2011 flood.

I hope that present day Amite County families continue to swim in both the east and west forks. The Amite River was a great source of inexpensive family fun for those of us who grew up here. While back home, we see it now and think wistfully to when we were young and loved going to the river!

*Chapter 5*

## PRAYERFUL THINKING AND MORE

### A SINFUL PRAYER ANSWERED

THANK YOU, LORD, for letting me grow up in Amite County, Mississippi, a part of the Bible Belt, and for the money you allowed me to deposit in your spiritual bank. Money that I've had to withdraw on occasion to tide me over!

People who didn't go to church as youngsters may not understand that religious education has its fun side. Some of the most humorous things I've ever encountered were at church.

We are taught that anything we want is achievable, through earnest prayer. This morning I had breakfast at a café counter and sat next to a Christian man. We struck up a conversation. He told me he had recently prayed a sinful prayer and that it was answered.

Across the street from that restaurant is a lake, a large one. There is a swimming area. The water has not yet warmed up a lot as it will do later this summer. His church does not have a baptismal but uses the lake for that purpose.

Not long ago, his church had eight baptisms scheduled on a cool Sunday morning. Another church had three and the two different pastors had combined their service. My breakfast companion is a deacon who assists. His first duty was to walk into the lake and pinpoint the spot where the water was deep enough, but not too deep, to baptize. He placed a marker pole at that spot.

He then accompanied each of the converts out to their respective preacher and stood alongside, walking them back to shore as well. He explained that his church could put in a baptismal but believes that service should be conducted outdoors as a witness to non-believers whom they hope to convert.

At least, he said, many fishermen headed out for a day on the lake notice what is going on, and act courteously with boat speeds, coming and going to the dock, etc.

My new friend said the water was cold enough that about halfway through the ceremony he began to earnestly pray that it would soon be over. He said he prayed no one would see what was happening and delay the service, so he could more quickly return to dry land, and warmth!

His prayer was answered, he said, as no one came forward and he was soon back in regular clothing. He said he now regretted praying for that outcome. We both laughed and agreed, yes, it is funny sometimes just what we do ask for!

## SUMMER FUN

Summer's coming! What did that thought mean to a child growing up in Amite County during the 1940s to 1960s? It was an exciting time!

The school term, at least through the 1950s, was eight and not nine months long. School days started just after Labor Day, in early September. They were done around the end of April. There were four solid months of "no school"!

For boys, at least, it meant a lot of barefootin'. Leaving the shoes aside. One had to be careful crossing pastures, watching for critters like snakes but also for the infernal sticker. If a patch of stickers was encountered, it was akin to working your way through a military minefield. One had to be careful about stepping on rocks if near a gravel road; wary of a hot surface if near a paved one.

Two of my aunts married military men. One lived in Pennsylvania, the other in Kentucky. Summer was a time when your first cousins from out of the area came for an extended visit or you went to see them. I don't recall vacations as such. It seemed as if your parents worked around the year with no time or money for extended vacations.

But the 'cousin visit' thing in either direction gave your family a chance to visit, often a chance to return home to see mother and father, grandparents, aunts and uncles.

Getting out of school at the end of April for farm kids meant a return to field chores – planting, picking cotton, watermelons. And it said that swimming season was back! Muddy ponds with their mysterious warm and cold spots; your nearby spring-fed (and very cold) creek; the Amite River on Sunday afternoons, swinging into the water on the rope in the tree, waiting to eat that watermelon cooling in the river itself. Some beginning flirting going on too! It was a social place as well as swimming hole.

For the town kids, too, it could mean the beginning of your work experiences. I sold watermelons for my uncle alongside Highway 24. Picked cotton for him a season or two. Some children's folks owned stores and one might work there during the summer. I remember setting up a shoeshine wagon, and working at the ice plant in Liberty which my father owned.

The memories of summer in Mississippi! Looking back, a great time of no school, swimming, what we called work but would later find had been no work really but just an experiment in beginning to do so.

And the amazing part of this, compared to today's world - it was all done without air conditioning, when one was lucky to have Mother Nature's rare breeze or the luxury of the new co-op's electricity which powered a fan!

## RESOLVE TO RESOLVE

Have you made your New Year's resolutions? I'm still considering mine. A good one would be to lose a few pounds, but I haven't resolved to diet so it may not happen. I do great with diets until I get hungry and then my diet focus turns from today until tomorrow.

How did this resolution business start?

Historians believe New Year's resolutions can be traced back thousands of years to the ancient Babylonians, who lived in a region of Mesopotamia now known as Iraq. At the dawn of a new year, the Babylonians would promise their gods that they would return objects they borrowed and pay any debts they did not repay in the previous year.

Babylonians believed keeping these promises would bring them the gods' favor in the year ahead.

Romans later adopted a similar practice, promising Janus, their god of beginnings and endings, that they would conduct themselves well in the coming year. Depictions of Janus typically include two faces, which are meant to symbolize his link to both the past (looking back) and the future (looking ahead).

Early Christians also had a tradition similar to New Year's resolutions, as they would spend the first day of the New Year reflecting on mistakes they made in the past and resolving to improve themselves and avoid making such mistakes in the future.

I do resolve to enjoy some traditional Southern good luck dishes on New Year's Day, like black-eyed peas, collard greens, ham, and cornbread. Not a very good start to losing that weight, is it?

However you resolve to do it, have a Happy New Year!

## BROTHER, CAN YOU SPARE A DIME (STORE)?

Having lunch recently at a favorite restaurant in Florida, I read a plaque outside the building. It recognized the location as formerly housing the "Dime Store".

It's a little scary when history and your memory coincide, but so be it. My mind took me back to the Dime Store in Liberty in the late 1940s and 1950s. It was across the street from where Morgan's Small Engine Repair is now.

It was an affordable place where a boy or girl growing up was likely to find a toy to their liking. It was a place that fostered Christmas dreams. Yes, there was Sears and J. C. Penney's and Montgomery Ward's and Western Autos, usually in other places, but the Dime Store was in Liberty, at hand.

During the year, it was the place you went to for a model balsawood airplane (cost, 10 cents) or if you were a girl, I guess, maybe a book of paper dolls (cost, 10 cents). You could go to the movie theatre with a quarter, use 10 cents to get in, and instead of paying a nickel each for a Coke, popcorn, and a candy bar, one could save a dime and drop by the Dime Store afterwards.

If I recall correctly, a penny's tax didn't start until the 12 cent mark so something that cost a dime, cost a dime only.

As Christmas grew closer, so did the stock of Good Things at the Dime Store!  Walking through there and seeing them interfered with one's sleep, because it was harder to get to sleep at night thinking about them. Imagining a favorite under the Christmas tree!

The only competitor in Liberty for my Christmas dream world was the M & T Store, which was next door to the Barber Shop. At Christmastime, Lionel trains made their appearance. Candies only available during the holidays showed up there too. I especially remember those kind of hard but chewable ones with the white centers and chocolate covering.

Miss Vera Robertson worked there and tolerated my staying in the M & T Store too long, staring at those trains. I always remember her kindness towards me.

For today's child, what's the equivalent of the Dime Store? I suppose it's Walmart or on a smaller scale, a Dollar General or Family Dollar store. Children now probably want an IPhone instead of a toy. But the only thing constant in life is change, and we have to learn to accept such things.

My hope is that when they reach my age down the line, they have the pleasant memories I do of a would-be Dime Store, M & T Store, or whatever other places now help them enjoy the unique nature of Christmas.

Merry Christmas, everyone!

## SUPPORT YOUR NEWSPAPER

Are you like me? The transmission in your mind is stuck in Neutral when it should be in Drive, and isn't helping you move forward with a Christmas gift idea for those who "have everything"?

Consider this. A gift subscription to the Wilk-Amite Record. It's a gift that will last all year, and if the person you purchase it for already is a subscriber, they'll get a year added onto their current account.

It's likely the person you're shopping for either lives here or maybe grew up here and has an interest in what's happening locally, so your gift will be appreciated.

Greg Adams and those who help him are doing a good job with the paper. It's not an easy job and it's not a cheap job. All costs go up. During my tenure as owner and publisher during 2011 and 2012, no costs were reduced.

Newspapers like the Wilk-Amite Record and the Southern Herald in neighboring Liberty are becoming fewer nationally as things like social media increase. But social media isn't for all of us. Personally, I like to hold my news source in my hands. If I'm reading a book, I like it held in my hands rather than on a computer screen, even a small one.

The Southern Herald is the county's oldest business, and the Wilk-Amite Record is the second oldest, in business since 1892. In 2017, just really a year away, the Wilk-Amite Record celebrates 125 years! Be a part of that celebration and the continuation of a local institution dedicated to you, the resident and the reader.

Call (601) 225-9200 today to start your gift subscription(s) or even your own. No one said you can't give yourself a gift. Or send your name and address with a $40 check to Wilk-Amite Record, PO Box 130, Gloster MS 39638. It's $45 for an out of state subscription. If the cost sounds high, think of it as four hamburgers eaten out at a fast food place, compared to receiving Amite and Wilkinson county news at your home 52 weeks in a row!

Credit card payments are accepted too. Be a little patient with the phone, since the staff is small and sometimes out of the office covering a meeting or other event; perhaps at the post office mailing out the papers; or delivering those sold over the counter at local stores. Leave a message and someone will call you back. E-mails to newsdesk@wilkamiterecord.com are welcome, too.

We hope your Christmas is merry and your New Year is happy and successful, and thank you for your continued support of YOUR newspaper, the Wilk-Amite Record!

# Chapter 6

---

# Cars, Cops, Football
# and a Mystery

### DRIVING THE OLD FORD

DURING THIS FAST moving year of 2015, 1935 seems so long ago and indeed 80 years have passed. So what, you say? Well, a car was made in 1935 that is forever lodged in my memory.

In 1957, my sister and I returned to Amite County from Oregon. Our folks stayed out west for the summer to close down our life there. My sister was starting college at Blue Mountain, Mississippi, in the fall. I was ready for the 9th grade. She and I stayed in our grandparents' homes near Liberty.

Carrie and Ernest Rice had the pleasure of my sister's company, while Susie and Pollard Anders were stuck with me. I was 14, and cars – and girls – were on my mind. My Grandfather Anders had a 1935 Ford four-door sedan. It was his baby. He hadn't owned it many years, and had probably paid a couple hundred dollars. He was fussy about that car.

Reluctantly, I'm certain, he allowed me to learn how to drive. Driver's license? Insurance? You gotta be kidding. I was permitted to go to Liberty to buy groceries and run other errands. My first forays into the "big city" didn't allow me to cross Main Street, Highway 24. I parked on the gravel lot behind the M&T Store, a lot that still exists though the store building changed names long ago.

There were numerous adventures associated with driving. Running off into a ditch – the day the stick shift came unscrewed and pulled out of the floor – overheating and pulling over to carefully add water to the radiator – and so on. And yes, I was a young boy, and on occasion snuck out to the Tastee Freeze. But fortunately nothing serious happened. In return, I cleaned and polished it for my granddad, and he liked that part.

My grandfather died in the early 1960s and my dad inherited the Ford, but it made him sad to have it so he sold it. Does it still exist? I wonder. The chances are slim, but it may be around in a collection. I hope so. Certainly some great memories would ebb out of me to see it again.

In 2015, from the Gillsburg Road, I still look over and see the tiny little one-car garage it was kept in and I'm glad it still remains. It looks a little lonely but seems to be well maintained and I thank today's owners of that property for that.

A few days ago, in Florida, I saw a For Sale ad for a 1936 Ford. In '36, a hump was added to the trunk space for more room, so collectors know that edition as the humpback model. The flat-head V-8 was also increased from 60 hp to 85 hp. Otherwise the cars are basically alike. The asking price was $17,500. Holy moly! Way out of my "toy price" range. But I called. I was up-front with the owner. I wasn't a buyer, I explained, but would like to take a few photos of his car and write a short story about it.

*Doc Johnson's 1936 Florida Ford.*

Doc Johnson, who inherited the Ford from his father, offered to take me for a ride, but I declined, thinking it wasn't fair to waste his time and gasoline on a non-purchaser. It was great to look, though. Doc's car still has the original interior, now 79 years old, and it's in very good condition. The memories flooded back as I looked from behind the windshield – checked out the small dashboard – looked at that stick shift stuck in the middle of the floor. Doc's courtesy was much appreciated!

## MYSTERY AT ROSELAND

The people of Amite County are respectful of cemeteries. For the most part, burial places are kept neat and clean. The grounds at Robinson Baptist Church in Peoria are one good example. My parents and many relatives and old friends and acquaintances have their final resting place there, and across all the years I've visited, I've never been there when it has been overgrown or otherwise neglected.

As a child, I played in and around the Liberty cemetery. Not around the headstones or on the grass, but bike riding on the roads was commonplace. Most often it was the best direct route to get to Tan Yard Creek where I'd do a little exploring.

I've been told of an instance where an old cemetery was on private property and wasn't wanted, and headstones were bull-dozed down. Call me a coward but I wouldn't want to arrive at the Pearly Gate with a driving record that included having driven a Caterpillar over tombstones.

Arriving in Gloster several weeks ago, I took my usual turn off Highway 24 by H & H Lumber and drove by Roseland

Cemetery. I glanced over to quickly look at my Great Uncle John Anders' plot. I didn't see the headstone but kept going, just thinking I'd looked too late and had missed it.

*Roseland Cemetery, Gloster, Mississippi.*

A couple of weeks later, same turn, same route, same result. This time I looked more carefully, and sure enough, the tombstone wasn't in sight. That seemed odd. So I turned around, drove back, and walked to his burial site. The stone was there, all right, but was laying on its side. Something or someone had knocked it over.

The base wasn't completely level but seemed level enough so that the top part of the monument wouldn't have just toppled over. If a wind came along that blew that heavy rascal over, I'm glad I wasn't out and about in the weather. It also did not appear that the structure had been struck by such as a mower. Did someone topple it? I really don't think so, and honestly couldn't figure out why it wasn't where it was supposed to be.

In Gloster, I rest easy knowing that Mrs. Monzella Tickles, town clerk, will help me with such matters. I have confidence in her abilities and the way she does her job. She called Gary Sterling, Gloster's maintenance superintendent, who drove to Roseland and met me there. The two of us together couldn't come up with a cause.

Just one of life's little mysteries.

But Mr. Sterling was very helpful and promised to get the tombstone back in the upright position. I haven't been back since but you know what? I believed him and am certain that Great Uncle John Anders now rests easier with a straight up and down marker. Mr. Sterling struck me as a get-'er-done kind of guy and I appreciate how both he and Mrs. Tickles quickly came to my rescue.

Thank you, Town of Gloster! You are appreciated.


**GEAUX TIGERS!**

Who in their right mind would be a LSU fan? Guess that goes a long way to explain why I am.

I really don't like the Alabama Crimson Tide. What does that mean, crimson tide? Sounds like a river of blood. The LSU Tigers would probably agree with that after the game I watched two plays of last night.

I suppose living in North Stadium during my college days, the north end of Tiger Stadium, cemented my demented loyalty. We were all so broke. Looking out onto Mike the Tiger's cage, we were jealous of the generous hunks of meat tossed in there.

Why didn't Mike have to do with Ramen Soup like the rest of us? Peanut butter and crackers, stale bread? He would have appreciated college more. For sure he would have appreciated leaving there, getting a job, and eating better.

I was convinced all along that LSU's achievements this year were overrated, that going to Alabama to play was like a Christian foolishly volunteering to take on lions and tigers in the Roman coliseum. With a pocket knife. Nick Saban draws my ire. He had it made at LSU, defaulted to the NFL to make some really big bucks as if he didn't make enough already, and giving it up on success there, went the traitor route and returned to the Crimson Tide.

That's a politically incorrect name, now, by the way. Too violent. They should be renamed something like – hmmm? – how about the Daisy Petals? Just one idea. A kinder, gentler team would be a good idea, especially when they come to Tiger Stadium or we have to go over there.

Actually, the people of Alabama are okay. They're pretty much just like us, except for one thing. They root for the wrong football team. This latest result is living proof of that.

Nothing works me up like a Tiger football game. Can any one team figure out more creative ways to either lose or to make a game close that should be a runaway? So I opted to watch a movie with my wife instead, to keep my blood pressure under control. I'd had to have EMS come to my house and remark: "Yep, just another Tiger fan. No great loss." Which is what a Florida EMS team would say.

Don't get me into talking about the Gators, please.

The two times I switched over to the ball game...first time, LSU was something like 3rd down and 25 on their own five yard line, and the Alabama defense was salivating so hard, Leonard Fournette, who for once had less than a look of confidence stenciled on his face, couldn't get any traction for all the drool on the field. Thirty-one yards, yeah man.

The second time, Alabama's defense was chasing our quarterback so furiously, he looked like a mouse on a Saturday night trying to get out of a crowded Texas bar without harm.

By the time this appears in the Wilk-Amite Record, LSU would have had to face Arkansas, probably Ole Miss, and maybe even Texas A&M. Nothing is easy in the SEC.

The only way LSU can get out of this mess is to somehow face Alabama in the playoffs, win, and laugh all the way home.

Am I betting large amounts of money on that? What did I say about being out of my mind at the start of this story? I'd better try to redeem myself and keep my money in my thin little wallet.

Nevertheless, and I can't help myself…Geaux Tigers!

## JAMMING

Do you like traffic jams? Growing up around here, they were very infrequent. Maybe on a football night, especially if everyone was traveling to an out of town game at the same time.

Travel this country a bunch, drive through cities like Los Angeles (probably the worst); Atlanta (certainly in the competition); and Houston (a contender, for sure) and you'll find some traffic jams.

It's always interesting when you're driving Interstate 10 purposefully during "off hours" and encounter a four or five mile backup…single lane ahead…construction…replacing a bridge so you're not inconvenienced…double traffic fines ahead where workers are taking a nap, etc.

The only time you might encounter an annoying amount of traffic on MS Highway 24 is either when work lets out in McComb…or when Walmart has a big sale. I don't mean it's safe out there, but at least the amount of traffic is generally not unmanageable.

But someone can take the worse concept and make something good out of it, can't they? Hey, that's the American way.

Have you ever eaten a traffic jam?

Recently, in a Florida fruit stand, I (of the Sweet Tooth Anders clan) was searching the jams and jellies. There's a large display from The Dutch Kettle of Hamptonville, North Carolina. Hey, what's this? I thought. Sounds good!

Homemade Style Traffic Jam…well, jam. Now whatever this column is, it isn't a cooking or food show. But Traffic Jam? Caught my eye. It's a concoction of strawberries, blueberries, and red raspberries. So I opted for a 19 ounce Mason jar of the stuff.

Finished off the last bit of it this morning, on top of a couple of large catheads. Catheads being biscuits, of course, but you knew that. Mmmmm mmmmm good! Well, all good things must end, but my trips up what's called The Nature Coast of Florida, State Highway 19 that parallels the west coast, hopefully aren't ending, and that's where the fruit stand is.

If I'm just lucky, real lucky, there will be some sort of traffic jam on Highway 19 that will cause me to just have to stop at the fruit stand again. For Traffic Jam jam, of course…while not to forget the pecan pieces that I'm always encouraged to bring home, back to my wife. Pecan pie ain't bad, either.

Life is good! Thank you Lord.

## COPPING OUT SOMEPLACE ELSE

Recently, while traveling in upstate New York, I stopped for breakfast in Bainbridge, NY. My quest is always for local restaurants of the "mom and pop" variety, and the S & S Café was no exception. It was in the old downtown area, and obviously a favorite of locals on a Sunday morning.

While waiting for my bacon and eggs (grits are pretty much out of the question in that area), I perused a small newspaper of the Wilk-Amite Record variety. The following historical article caught my eye. Troop C of the New York State Police is headquartered at nearby Unadilla, NY.

"Troop C was established in 1921 with Captain Daniel Fox appointed as Troop Commander. A temporary headquarters was established at the Central Hotel, Sidney, NY, until the construction of a new facility could be completed.

1917 Trooper requirements were as follows. Applicants were required to be United States Citizens, pass a physical and mental examination, be of good moral character, between age twenty-one and forty, at least five feet eight inches tall and weigh not less than 140 pounds. He also must have been honorably discharged from the military.

On June 11, 1917, 420 applicants from a list of 1592 appeared at the Executive Chamber, Albany, NY, to take the written examination for 232 allotted positions. Only 168 passed.

A second examination was given on July 2, 1917, to 542

applicants with only 62 passing. Many applicants were eliminated because of no horsemanship experience. Those that passed the written examination were examined for physical defects.

Trooper enlistments were for two year time periods with resignations requiring approval of the Superintendent. Troopers were on call 24 hours a day with an occasional 24 or 48 hour leave after an extended duty. They were given a two week winter vacation."

It's interesting to note that good horse sense was as important back then as it should be now!

# Chapter 7

# Pickups, Guns,
# and Grand Thoughts

## BACK IN A PICKUP

BACK IN THE Day, riding in the back of a pickup was as natural as apple pie in Amite County. Although without doubt there must have been some accidents, no one thought much about the practice. Often it was a Sunday afternoon thing, just riding around, maybe going to or from the swimming hole on the Amite River.

Anyway it was your dad who was driving, and most likely he wouldn't be messing around – drinking – driving too fast with his child or children in the bed of the pickup. And your mom was up there in the cab with him to keep it all in line.

We didn't all the federal rules back then that made the practice illegal or at least not recommended. Here's a current (October 2015) quote from the Insurance Institute for Highway Safety:

"Federal standards require that occupant compartments of vehicles be designed to protect occupants during a crash. The beds of pickup trucks are designed to carry cargo, not people, and are not designed to provide protection in a crash. In addition, children and adults can be easily ejected from cargo areas at relatively low speeds as a result of a sharp turn to avoid an obstacle or crash."

The Institute goes on to say: "The hazards of riding in cargo areas have been addressed in 30 states and the District of Columbia by a variety of laws, most of which are designed to protect children, but few of which provide comprehensive protection for all children younger than 16. Safety belt and child restraint laws also may apply to prevent people from riding unrestrained in cargo areas."

In the olden days, most of our roads were gravel and Interstates were a long way off, both in distance and existence. The trucks (and cars) of yesteryear went slower, speed limits were lower.

Where does Mississippi stand on the subject? I didn't check state law but according to the Insurance Institute, it's one of the 20 states that have no restrictions on riding in a pickup bed.

I'm in Amite County frequently and it's been quite a while, though, since I've seen any kids or even adults doing so. Most of my travel, admittedly, is on roads like Highway 24. And that shoulder-less rascal can be dangerous enough while confined to a pickup's cab and strapped in. I'm guessing that the practice of unrestrained pickup bed riding does take place on country roads.

It's a fond memory, regardless. The wind in your hair, the occasional bug in your teeth, sort of an early motorcycle-type feeling. And those of us who were boys could imagine being behind the wheel later on, an event that often started with driving the old Ford in the hay field.

For girls like my sister, who were thinking of what her real or imagined boyfriend might think of her, the fun of riding in the back of a pickup had gone away by about age 13. It was a horrendous thought to even take a chance that "he" might see you in such a place. It just wasn't lady-like.

The real professional pickup bed riders even installed – or their dads did – an old seat facing backwards behind the cab. Now that was the place to be! The only living creature that enjoyed being in the back more than a young boy was a dog. A dog could ride for hours with its nose stuck out into the wind, its ears flying backwards. With their sharp sense of smell, a cross-country trip must have been a dream come true!

## THINGS WERE GRAND IN GRAND GULF

Returning to Amite County from Vicksburg recently, I had a couple of hours to spare and planned to drive around Port

Gibson. That little town has a fascinating history and is well kept and a pleasure to visit.

Driving south on Highway 61, though, still north of Port Gibson, I saw the sign pointing the way to Grand Gulf Military Monument, and noted it was only seven miles west of my route. It is a place I had not previously seen, so I took the opportunity.

But for history's events, it seems, Grand Gulf may well have been the state capital of Mississippi. There had been talk of just that. At one time it was a thriving community of 1,000 people with two newspapers, a hospital, numerous businesses including theatres, a school, and several churches. Twenty (20) steamboats stopped weekly. King Cotton was hauled to the wharf, even a small train was built to transport cotton to the river for shipment north.

Then across time came...yellow fever...a devastating tornado...and the willy-nilly attitude of the Mississippi River which changed course and swept away 55 city blocks! When the Civil War started, only 158 people still lived in Grand Gulf.

Union General U. S. Grant occupied the town twice, essentially burning all the buildings by the second time. Grant tried to cross Union troops but was repelled by well-prepared Confederates during a huge battle, primarily between artillery on-shore and gunboats on the river. Grant's forces retreated to below Grand Gulf, to Bruinsburg west of Port Gibson, where they crossed with less resistance. And you know the rest of that story.

Not many towns have had the ups and downs of Grand Gulf, and it's a fascinating place to visit yet. The museum is open 7 days a week from 8 to 5, except for major holidays. A lady from Port Gibson who was working as a volunteer in the gift shop knew of the late and well-known Liberty resident Mr. Sam Roberts so we had an interesting discussion about that family.

There's a nice RV park and my intention, written on my mental bucket list, is to go back for a longer stay. Next week, if the Good Lord is willing and the Creek don't rise, I'll tell you of a nice little story I learned of in the museum display. Meanwhile, plan to visit Grand Gulf, Mississippi, yourself, a very nice day trip from Amite County.

## WEAPON OF WAR, WEAPON OF PEACE

Last week I wrote about a visit to Grand Gulf Military Monument Park near Port Gibson, Mississippi. While there I spent time browsing the museum.

In a display case stood a Spencer rifle for the viewing. Attached to the rifle was a story about it and its owner during the Civil War.

Here's a bit of background on the Spencer rifle from Wikipedia, the Internet encyclopedia.

"The **Spencer repeating rifle** was a manually operated lever-action seven shot repeating rifle produced in the United States by three manufacturers between 1860 and 1869. Designed by

Christopher Spencer, it was fed with cartridges from a tube magazine in the rifle's buttstock.

The Spencer repeating rifle was adopted by the Union Army, especially by the cavalry, during the American Civil War, but did not replace the standard issue muzzle-loading rifled muskets in use at the time. The **Spencer carbine** was a shorter and lighter version."

Back to my story. The Spencer on display is a .50 caliber carbine. One can only imagine the excitement of a young soldier in 1863 on being issued such an improved weapon, with which he could fire up to 20 rounds in a minute. So it was a hopeful young Union infantryman who was unloaded from a steamboat in the Mississippi River, sent to assault Confederate forces in rifle pits atop the rocky head of Grand Gulf in 1863.

But I learned long ago in police work that the fun of having a firearm goes away when the other fellow has one too. So fate had it that the young soldier was struck by a round fired by a Rebel, in a Southern farmer's field. The soldier's rifle fell beside him.

His wound was serious. But we in the South are a compassionate people, and the farmer and his family found him and took him home, attempting to save his life. Alas, their efforts came to naught, and he died. The rifle was put away. A letter in his pocket with his family's name in Indiana was saved.

No communication was possible or attempted during the war, but at its conclusion in 1865, the Southern family wrote a letter, explaining the circumstances of his death and giving the place of his burial. It was in no remote location, but in their family plot. The Indiana family came to Grand Gulf, exhumed their young son's body, and took him home for burial in their own family cemetery.

They left the Spencer rifle as a gesture of appreciation. And it came to this day to be displayed at Grand Gulf, not far from where its owner fell in battle.

A visit to Grand Gulf, Mississippi, will provide you the chance to learn the touching story of this rifle, and probably of many others. Coincidentally, during my visit, a couple from New York State - Bob and Judy – were touring the park which seems a miniature of Vicksburg. We had a great conversation about life in the South, both now and in earlier times, and as with the Indiana family during 1865, there was no animosity. It was just a friendly visit between like-aged fellow citizens of these United States. Isn't history a great teacher!

## BASS REEVES, A LAWMAN'S LAWMAN

Growing up in Amite County, Saturday afternoons were spent at the local theatre, watching Western movies. Guys like Gene Autry and Hopalong Cassidy were my heroes. I recall precisely the proud moment on my 10th birthday, near the ice plant in Liberty, when I strapped on a new double six-gun Roy Rogers rig.

Living out West in later life, in both New Mexico and Texas,

I became a fan of Western folklore surrounding gunfighters. People like Billy the Kid, Wyatt Earp, Doc Holliday and others. I once spent a day in Albuquerque, Texas, with a metal detector, searching for artifacts. Yes, Albuquerque, Texas, not New Mexico.

By then it was nothing but a spot in the woods, the only identifiable feature being a circular depression in the ground about 40 feet across where a hapless mule had gone round and round grinding the corn at a grist mill. John Wesley Hardin had been the sheriff there, he sometimes being on the good side of the law or the other, more often the other. Albuquerque, Texas, burned to the ground about 1905, having been abandoned after the railroad went around it and through nearby Cuero instead.

Dime novels of the late 1800s made certain gunfighters well known. One of the best was more or less by-passed by history. He was a lawman and his name was Bass Reeves.

Reeves was born in Arkansas on a plantation, probably the son of the owner, in 1838. During the Civil War, he fled into Indian Territory – now Oklahoma - and lived amongst three Indian tribes, learning their languages and the lay of the land. He married and eventually fathered 10 children.

In 1875, a rich man, Isaac Parker, was appointed federal judge of the lawless Indian Territory, the home of Robber's Roost and numerous other hideouts of owl hoots – outlaws – who dodged the law there. Occupants of Indian Territory were among the worst civilization had to offer. Two hundred deputy U. S.

Marshalls were hired to tackle the problems. (Fewer than 100 survived.)

U. S. Marshall James Fagan had heard of Reeves, a poor man, and recruited him. Bass Reeves became one of the best of the deputies, if not the best. During his career, he arrested more than 3,000 felons and was involved in 14 shootouts, killing his opponent in each. He had his hat shot off and was hit in the belt buckle but was never injured by gunfire. He was often alone, but had a firm belief and attitude that a bullet would not touch him.

Reeves' usual tactic was to let his opposite rush to fire the first shot, turning himself sideways to offer the smallest profile possible and to use his Winchester, not his six gun, to carefully aim and win. Like a careful, patient dueler.

He often worked undercover, riding into a cow camp or hideout, posing as an owl hoot himself, someone on the run, looking for work as a cowboy. It was an effective ruse, but at times he was recognized. His reputation had preceded him.

Earlier I said "probably the son of the owner". You see, Bass Reeves was a black man, born into slavery, and it's thought possible he was the illegitimate son of the plantation owner. As a youngster, he was given special privileges including taking care of the plantation's armory, its collection of firearms. He became a firearms expert and quite the marksman. He ran away after a dispute with the owner's son, and that's how he wound up in Indian Territory.

Bass Reeves was a fearless law officer. He was the first African-American deputy west of the Mississippi River. He himself was once charged with murdering a posse cook, and was tried in Judge Parker's court in Ft. Smith. He was acquitted, and at the conclusion of the trial, Judge Parker said: "Well, Bass, are you ready to go back to work?" Reeves did, immediately. Judge Isaac Parker, a rich white man, and Bass Reeves, a poor black man, respected each other and became very good friends.

One of Reeves' sons, Bennie, was charged with murdering his wife. Marshall Reeves was shaken by the incident but insisted on handling the arrest himself, and tracked Bennie down and brought him to justice in Ft. Smith. Bennie Reeves served time in Ft. Leavenworth, then lived the rest of his life as a responsible and model citizen.

When Oklahoma became a state in 1907, Bass Reeves, then 68, became an officer of the Muskogee, Oklahoma, police department. Was life perfect for him? No. He was largely restricted to being an officer in black areas of the town. But he was respected by his peers as were few others. In 1912, a bronze statue of Reeves was put on display in Pendergraft Park in Ft. Smith, Arkansas.

Bass Reeves had sometimes worked Indian Territory with an Indian guide. Some historians believe the fictional characters of the Lone Ranger, wearing a black mask, and Tonto, his faithful Indian sidekick, are based on the exploits of Reeves and his partner.

*Deputy U. S. Marshall Bass Reeves, 1838 – 1909.*

If Bass Reeves were alive today, and a lawman in Amite County, Mississippi, I'm guessing we'd have two or three fewer murderers of Gloster citizens on the loose. He didn't worry about his pension or Social Security because there weren't any. He just faithfully did his job to make where he worked a lawful, safe place. He never worried about being popular.

He died at age 71 of Bright's Disease and is buried in Muskogee. The next time I'm near that area, I'll seek out his gravesite to pay homage to that courageous police officer of yesteryear.

# Chapter 8

———❧———

# HEALTH TO WEATHER
# AND IN BETWEEN

## LIVING WELL, LIVING LONG

THE FOLLOWING WAS sent to me by a friend in Texas. I'd gladly credit the author if I knew who wrote it. It's important information for all Wilk-Amite Record readers.

### Exercise and Quality of Life

A recent study interviewed 700 people living in England who all had brain scans when they reached the age of 73. Three years earlier they had taken a survey regarding their exercise level. People in the study who reported being the most physically active, tended to have larger brain volumes of gray and normal white matter which is an indication of less brain deterioration. Regular exercise also appeared to protect against the formation of white matter lesions, which are linked to thinking and memory decline.

Going to the gym is not the only way to exercise. Gardening, cleaning the car, walking at a moderate pace, and dancing count. Studies also show that even those starting late-in-life exercises have about a seven fold reduction in their risk of becoming ill or infirmed after eight years than those that remain sedentary.

People who drink one sugary drink a day (like one Coke) are 80 times more likely to become a diabetic in old age. Those of us who work in health care in this part of the country often see what we refer to as MFID or Mexican Food Induced Diabetes.

Successful aging means more than simply remaining alive. It involves minimal disability, little or no serious chronic disease diagnoses, depression, cognitive decline or physical infirmities that would prevent someone from living independently. Not that money makes you happy, but having greater economic resources means you can afford to seek preventative treatments and eat healthy.

The longest living person, a woman in France, lived to 120 and was independent until she was 110. She swam daily and ate the Mediterranean diet (including red wine in moderation). In addition she had a circle of friends who kept her involved in society.

Remember if you don't want to live in a nursing home, you can decrease the odds of having to do so by exercising and eating healthy.

## BEATING THE RATS

Growing up in Amite County, we were encouraged to go into the world and achieve, to accomplish. And rightfully so, it seems. I moved away from Liberty after the sixth grade, finishing that year in the building that is now Blaylock's Grocery Store.

Family and work travels took me to Oregon, Louisiana, Arizona, Texas and New Mexico, not to mention a year in Thailand during the Vietnam War.

Across time I acquired three boys, spaced just five years apart, oldest to youngest. While they were growing up, career ladders stood in front of me, challenging me to climb them, and I worked hard at it. Sometimes demands imposed were at the expense of my children, though I was trying to give them a better life.

Not to say I didn't participate in their activities or take them camping or otherwise try to be a good father, but looking back I can see more could have been done. When my youngest son was 10, my daughter was born.

Maybe it was my Southern upbringing, but somehow I was motivated to take more interest in her young life. Maybe I was just trying to be protective. But wanting to be more involved, and make up too for some lost time with my sons, I backed away from career achievement though I continued to work and support my family.

Yes, I made a conscious decision to downshift and did and life changed, for the better. My daughter was good in academics but was also a gifted athlete. Where did that come from? It wasn't from me. She won a state championship in New Mexico in track and field, throwing the discus. She finished second in the state in shot put. She was skilled enough in volleyball to earn an athletic scholarship to college, and graduating fifth in her high school class was important in that regard, too.

And with her, I got to see it all from the front row.

I'm proud but not bragging because being more involved with her school things and her life made me regret not having done more of that with my sons. We had and still have good relationships but could it have been better, could I have done a more quality job?

As we work and accomplish, we look down the road and see the light at the end of the tunnel – retirement – and we hope it's not the train coming. Now I'm 10 years down the road from having passed the light and can look back through that tunnel in the opposite direction.

What I see is an insightful reflection of a life lived during which I could have provided a good enough living and perhaps have been a better father, by having made choices that seemed worse then but may have been a bit better in the long haul.

After all, every Indian tribe needs warriors, and not all chiefs, to get the job done. Live and learn.

Are you doing the best for your children and grandchildren? Making the best calls in that regard? In the long term, we have our God and our family. More time spent with each, while we have options, might be the wisest choice, rather than always trying to be the winning rat in the race.

## MAN'S BEST FRIEND

Dogs are as common in our world as, well, dogs. Many of us have one or more. From the ripe age of two, living in Liberty for me was sharing my world with Tokyo, my little part rat terrier. She came to our house as a stray and stayed 18 years.

The photo is me at age two with Tokyo in Liberty, near where the Sheriff's Office is now located. I was halfway through LSU when she passed away. She was probably an Ole Miss or State fan and I hope that didn't have anything to do with it. She was quite literally a member of our family.

One thing we notice about our dogs is how many of them react to bad weather. According to the Society for the Prevention of Cruelty to Animals, dogs can detect changes in barometric pressure and they even feel the static electric field that occurs during storms. They may become agitated or more excited when the barometric pressure lowers.

*Tokyo and the author, Liberty, Mississippi, 1945.*

Most of us have owned an animal or two that would hide under a bed or under our feet during unsettled conditions when thunder booms or lightning flashes, as if they think we can somehow protect them. Some dogs can sense storms that are still miles away.

Researchers at Penn State University found that between 15 and 30 percent of all dogs are very scared of thunder and probably experience a rapid increase of cortisol which is a stress hormone.

A dog's ability to smell is said to be 30,000 to 40,000 times that of humans and it's no surprise they can smell ozone in the air that's associated with lightning.

Like us older dog owners – older referring to owners and not to the dogs – dogs feel the effect of seasonal changes and have more stiffness and lameness during adverse weather, especially during cold or wet times. Just like us.

From the poor results I sometimes see when humans attempt to make forecasts, a dog with its inborn capabilities and a good obedience score at a Doppler weather radar school would be a highly prized pet!


## WEATHER OR NOT...

As a child in Amite County, I recall sitting on my grandparents' porch on the Gillsburg Road close to Liberty, watching violent summer thunderstorms.

One day lightning hit a big tree about 50 feet from the porch swing on which I was sitting, and which I quickly vacated after I watched a fireball race down that tree, splitting it in half. My hair was electrified. So was I!

On Sunday, August 31, 2008, I was in Baker, Louisiana, just down the road from Amite County. The forecast was for thunderstorms, winds 65 MPH or more, and up to 9 inches of rain over the next two or three days. A lady named Rita was coming to visit. Hurricane Rita. We all remember Katrina but I especially remember Miss Rita.

*My Great Uncle Christopher Robinson, 1943,*
*in front of the tree later struck by lightning, Gillsburg Road.*

My mother passed away on July 11, 2008. My sister and I in-herited her home and we were there in late August doing some cleaning and remodeling, preparing it for sale. Weather-wise, things were forecast to get rough on Monday, September 1$^{st}$, Labor Day. My sister did the wise thing and did the boogie-split for Texas early Sunday.

I thought I'd work until the last minute, retreat to my aunt's house near Gloster and wait out the storm, then return to Baker and do some more work. But I waited a minute or two too long.

The wind and rain got serious on Monday about noon. Between 1 PM and 7 PM it reached 90 MPH. Before I could leave, big oak trees blew down on both ends of the street. Like a rat, I was trapped. And there were electrical wires across the driveway.

I had no generator, and the only worst thing is having a bunch of neighbors who do so that you have to listen to the noise while not getting the benefit of the racket. The home is a brick home, not made for ventilation if the air conditioner isn't working. There was no fan.

By 1:30 PM on Monday, the electricity was off, and I had not even a radio to listen to hurricane news. I had three eggs in the refrigerator, which I opened as little as possible to conserve the cold and ice. Sleep that night was close to impossible. We had cleared the home of furniture and I was on the floor. On Tuesday I ate my eggs. The orange juice in the refrigerator had gone bad.

I had tap water, a few canned goods, and some bread and crunchy peanut butter. I normally don't like the crunchy kind but I did on Tuesday. There was some freshly-caught sac-a-lait in the freezer. I took it to neighbors who were hurricane-ready, thinking they'd invite me over when they cooked it. On Wednesday I smelled frying fish and walked over and they said: "Want some?"

Does a bear…? Well, you know. That was one of the best meals I ever had, along with the ice cold Coke they gave me. The rain, she kept on a'coming. By Wednesday night, my bread and peanut butter were gone. Finally on Thursday, the Baker city crews, who did just an excellent job, cleared the fallen oak trees from the street at the south end. I locked the house, drove over wires as if they weren't there, and was…gone to Texas!

Traveling west on Interstate 10, I vowed to stop at the first restaurant I saw that had electric lights showing, which meant the air conditioner would be working. It was the Waffle House in Crowley, Louisiana. The folks working there were tired of the hot, humid weather too and it was meat-locker cold inside.

Seven years later, I have great memories when I pass that Waffle House and of the air-conditioned meal I had, and often I stop in and relive them. If there had been a server there named Rita on Thursday, September 4th, 2008, though, I'd probably just keep on going.

*Chapter 9*

COOLING DOWN,
AND U.S. HIGHWAY 82

**THE LIBERTY ICE HOUSE REMEMBERED**

IN **1949**, MY father, George Davis Anders, built the Liberty Ice House. Bobby Lunsford and Dude Morgan of Liberty were two of the people who helped him. I do not remember who others were.

My mom, Lucille Rice Anders, and my dad also purchased the small brick house that today remains across Church Street from the ice plant. I was six and my sister, Faye Carol, was 10 at the time. We moved there from another house in Liberty and lived there until 1953.

*Amite County native Robert Lunsford - Redmond, Oregon, 2011.*

The ice plant is concrete block construction. When you face the building, you are looking west. There was a large concrete "porch" which at first was open. The porch was later enclosed on the north end. Refreshments like candy and soda pop were sold there. In those days, we didn't call soft drinks "soda pop". We just said cold drinks.

Cold drinks referred to Coca Cola or Coke, Pepsi, Dr. Pepper, 7-Up, and others like Nehi Grape and Orange. There was a large circular metal container in the little store area, much like a metal container you might see today in a field for water for livestock. The coldest cold drinks in town were sold at the Ice House, since a plentiful supply of ice was always available.

I especially remember ice cold Dr. Pepper. 10, 2 and 4 were on the label, and Dr. Pepper promoted the idea that you should have one at those times of day as a picker-upper. These drinks were all in glass bottles. The bottles were returned and picked up by the delivery trucks, and cleaned and reused at the plant which may have been in McComb. An ice cold Dr. Pepper would truly tickle your throat going down! Your hand got very cold just reaching in to fish one out.

Refrigeration was just coming along but wasn't universally available in rural areas. Nearly everyone in town in Liberty had a "modern" refrigerator, but electricity either wasn't available in the country or people had didn't yet have the money to buy refrigerators. They had ice boxes, a refrigerator-looking insulated storage box.

Ice was delivered on rural routes by the trucks from the ice plant, perhaps twice a week. A small block of ice in an ice box might last a rural family two or three days, and was a real treat. Of course, electricity and the nearly universal acquisition of refrigerators by rural families would eventually do in ice plants. I remember being at my grandparents' home when the ice truck would come around.

The central part of the Liberty ice plant held the freezing boxes. There was a winch on an I-beam which lifted the heavy boxes out of the freezing area. I recall the big containers holding a 300 lb block of ice. Once out of the freezing area, it would be chipped along indentation lines, dividing it into successively smaller blocks, perhaps down to 10 lbs. Heavy metal tongs were used to carry the ice around.

As a young boy between my ages 6 to 10, I'd deliver ice around Liberty in small blocks in a basket on my bicycle. Of course I had to hurry. As you can imagine, the best business was during summer and naturally the ice melted fast in the Mississippi heat, so there was no tarrying. I also had to get the order out quickly once the order was called in so that I would know the person would be home. I would collect on delivery but I recall receiving perhaps a quarter. Two of my best customers lived over by the Liberty cemetery.

To the right of the freezing area was the equipment room, with the ice-making machinery. The use of ammonia was extensive, and of course an ammonia leak was very dangerous. There were stairs that led down into that area, and without an escort, my folks forbid my playing around near the ammonia. On one occasion, there was a leak and a worker, a man from Peoria, was blinded or nearly so. My folks went to visit him and carry him food and other necessities for some years, as I remember going with them. I don't recall his name but it was the second house north of Robinson Baptist Church in Peoria, towards Highway 24.

On the south side of the ice plant, and there was a separate door there too, was the fish room. I would accompany my father to Lake St. Mary where he would buy fish by the truckload. I remember going to the lake while the area was badly flooded. Back at the plant, the fish was kept under ice. Live frogs were also kept in a separate concrete enclosure in that room and sold as well. There was always a whole lot of croaking going on in the frog pen.

The Ice House was a central gathering place for my dad's friends, who would drop in to get a very cold "cold drink", and probably there were other liquids consumed there at least on the weekends. Amite County was officially "dry" in those days. I took a lot of teasing from the men who gathered there, but that was par for the course for a country boy then.

A lot of practical joking took place. Any device which contained something like those springs which jumped out of a box, having been touted as holding some dangerous animal, appeared at the ice house. It was a time when disagreements might be settled with an occasional fistfight, and I especially remember seeing one where someone was hit, went about 20 feet straight backwards before falling, being knocked out for a time.

One of the men who worked there was very sensitive to being "goosed". Touch him unexpectedly under the arm and he would turn around and start swinging, without looking at who he swung at. He was tormented in a friendly way with this, but if you goosed him, you'd better be ready to duck.

A man's word was his honor and many business deals were settled by a handshake, but violate that agreement and you might have the knuckles of that same man's hand in your face. Yet the police were seldom called, it was a time when you mostly handled your own problems.

Across the street from the Ice House and next to the little brick home was a grist mill where corn was ground. My dad also operated the grist mill. I have several memories of living in the brick house. One is the celebration of my 10th birthday when I got a Roy Rogers six-shooter set which I proudly wore to school, although my teacher made me take it off in the classroom. Somewhere I have a photo of my cowboy outfit and me in the back yard of that home.

My sister had a piano in the living room. She took lessons from Mrs. Harrison of Liberty for 11 years. Faye Carol and I had a white rabbit for a pet which had the run of the house. We also had our little dog Tokyo. One night we came home and a burglar was inside. My dad had a pistol handy and the burglar went out through the kitchen window and fled east towards the water tower, my dad in chase, but the would-be thief was not caught. Good thing for the burglar.

One day my mother, sister and I were sitting in our swing in the yard between the brick house and the grist mill. A mockingbird did a very unseemly thing which landed on my mother's head and we all had a great laugh about that – after she went inside and washed her hair!

Patsy Sharp who lived next door was a classmate at Liberty Elementary and she and I rode our bikes all over town and played "cops and robbers" to the extreme. There is a red fire plug near the cotton gin that was our rendezvous point and I think about our bike travels whenever I see it now. Liberty had open septic ditches by the ice plant in that day where wild onions grew and to this day I don't eat onions.

My dad sold the Ice House in 1953 when he went to Honduras with Mr. A. B. Williams as his millwright. My folks had built a new home on the Gillsburg Road about two and one half miles from town before my dad left to work out of country so they sold the little brick home in town too.

Thus my Liberty ice plant memories cover about a four year period of my life, but nevertheless it was a memorable time. My father owned a WWII surplus Jeep which was used in the business and kept by the side of the plant, and I sat in the Jeep and got to steer it a few times while "learning to drive".

A few years ago, I was in an ice plant in Florida that had been remodeled into a restaurant and I liked what I saw, and seriously thought about trying to acquire the Liberty Ice Plant and convert it into not a business but a residence. Life had other plans for me, though, and now at age 73, I doubt that will happen. But I have great memories of the time my dad built and operated the Liberty Ice Plant, and of growing up there as boy.

## NEVER FEEL BLUE ON U. S. HIGHWAY 82

My little 1956 Shasta travel trailer followed my truck and me through Liberty, Gloster and Centreville four days ago. Our destination was New Mexico and the start of a Bucket List item placed in the bucket during 2010.

At age 70, it's time to get it done. This project involves a cross-country trip on U. S. Highway 82. Its 1,700 miles begin at Brunswick, Georgia, next to the Atlantic Ocean; and end at the southernmost portion of the Rocky Mountains, near Alamogordo, New Mexico.

*1956 Shasta, my daughter Robyn in front,*
*Fredericksburg, Texas, 2013.*

Maybe you can get your kicks on Route 66, but you'll never feel blue on Route 82. With Chamber of Commerce support, I'll write a travelogue on the Highway 82 trip, and hope to have it published to promote RV travel to an area I called home for years.

Route 82 runs west from Georgia through Alabama, Mississippi, Arkansas, Texas, and New Mexico. It's truly an "ocean to the mountains" saga.

This road cuts through some pretty sizeable cities including Waycross and Albany, Georgia; Montgomery and Tuscaloosa, Alabama; and Texarkana, Wichita Falls and Lubbock, Texas. But I'm more interested in small town America, and there are not just a bucket full but a barrel full of little towns along the way.

Here in Mississippi, I'll visit Columbus, Starkville, Winona, Greenwood, Indianola and Greenville, not to mention the Glosters up that way. Normally, I won't seek out attractions more than 10 miles off the route, but Tupelo, 60 miles north of Columbus, will be an exception. I've never been to Elvis' hometown and want to see it.

A SPOT satellite tracker device will be used to send a daily e-mail to those interested in following the trip. It'll pinpoint my location on Google maps. If you'd like to receive this notification, send your e-mail address to me at DavisAndersMS@aim.com and I'll add you to the list. About 14 days will be spent on the road, and trip highlights will be published here over the next two or three editions. My wife has other commitments but will join me in Alabama or Georgia for the last week.

Starting in New Mexico makes it seem I'm doing the trip backwards. But that should save gas, since it'll be downhill all the way! Cloudcroft, New Mexico, near my departure point, has an elevation of 8,650 feet above sea level, while Brunswick, Georgia, where I'll finish, has the ocean at its doorsteps.

Come on. Let's take a deep breath of pure Rocky Mountain air on April 15th, and we'll end the trip a couple of weeks later by sticking our toes in the Atlantic Ocean. "Thank you" to God for the blessings which allow me to take such little adventures, and I pray He'll honor my request to have some special angels along.

*'56 Shasta and a big brother,*
*Atlantic Ocean, Brunswick, Georgia, 2013.*

Sometime I'll write about those angels. I think you'll appreciate them. Stay tuned!

# Chapter 10

———— ∞ ————

# CONDENSED DISCUSSIONS

## STILL DRIVING?

WE'RE ALL ON an incredible journey together in this world and no matter your age, that journey is called: "Getting Older."

Things reach a pivotal stage as we approach 70 as I'm doing now, at 69+. Changes take place. Someone wiser than I am has labeled this stage: The Golden Years. Frankly, I think somebody may have confused gold with silver, platinum or maybe even lead. But we press on.

Five (5) and zero (0) birthdays have always been the toughest, and the Big 7-Zero may take the cake, as we remember references in the Bible to three score and 10 and realize...heckfire, I'm there! Of course, if you're 80 or more, you think that 70 was a cake walk. Often I've thought: Who would want to live to be 100? Then it occurs to me to ask the person who's 99 that question and I believe I'd find an answer.

Those changes that take place...here's a few...hearing loss; body shape; hair and nails; hormone production; immunity; changes in organs, tissue and cells. Then there are changes in skin; sleep pattern; differences in the bones, muscles, and joints; and in the face.

I've tried to live a healthy lifestyle for the most part. Every now and then, maybe every three to six months, I just get a hankering for an ice cold beer but that's about my alcohol limit. I've never smoked since I inhaled more than my share of the second-hand stuff in Amite County, MS, in my early years, the window cracked an inch on the driver's side, as my lungs (like my mother's and my sister's were) cracked open a foot in a desperate search for fresh air.

Mrs. Ginny Wilkinson in Busy Corner News writes that she and a friend walk four miles each day and I applaud that. My wife and I do the same. Well, we walk an hour each day and it's about four miles. At any rate, between the Good Lord and good luck and a little effort, I don't have to take any medication and can still wrestle the occasional alligator, although now I limit myself to 7 foot or smaller alligators that have a strap around their jaws, and clipped toenails.

Still, those changes mentioned above persist. My loss of hearing is noticeable, not by me of course, but by others who don't speak up the way they should and who keep the doggone TV on too low and constantly are repeating things to my annoyance. Reading an advertisement recently that asked: Need better hearing? Take this test, answering yes or no...

___ You can hear, but you can't understand.
___ You are continually asking people to repeat themselves.
___ People say you play the radio or TV too loudly.

...I was proud of myself for scoring 100% until I realized it wasn't a good thing. Actually I know that already, and "sometime", I need to consider getting a hearing aid. Our hearing is complicated by things we did or had happen when younger, and mine is no exception. Once, I was cleaning my left ear with a bath cloth - so far so good - but it was wrapped around a rattail comb which slipped and punctured my eardrum, thus causing about a 10% loss in that ear. Later I flew helicopters for five years and during the first two or three didn't use proper hearing protection. And then there's just plain age - wear and tear - water down the river.

Seems to me, then, it might be interesting to take a look at these issues together over the next 10 or 12 weeks. I may even share my plan with you for my solution to the time-honored question: When should I stop driving? That's a lala-paloozer, isn't it?

Part I is somewhere else in the paper today. "%#&*@?" (Where?) you ask. "Sorry, I couldn't hear you. Will you stop whispering and speak up, please?" Don't worry, if it gets too hard, we'll chicken out and run some jokes instead.

# A CONDENSED STORY OF CONDENSED MILK

"Liberty. Founded 1809 and chartered 1828. Site of first Confederate monument in state, 1871. Here Gail Borden conducted condensed milk experiments. Dr. Tichenor's antiseptic was also originated here."

Thus says the historical waymark on Main Street at the northeast corner of the courthouse. Or it did. I've taken it so much for granted over so many years, I don't know if I've seen it there recently or not.

We all like to claim that such-and-such happened in our town. The other day, someone out West was discussing the Borden Company and I told them what I've always understood… that Gail Borden (he was actually Gail Borden Jr. as his father was Gail Borden)…well…conducted condensed milk experiments in Liberty. I may have said "invented" condensed milk in Liberty.

Fact or fiction? I'm certain someone in the Amite County Historical Society could expound on this. Meanwhile, I did some reading about Mr. Borden Jr.

From my youth, I seem to recall a small wooden house on Liberty's Main Street said to be the old Borden house. It was located between where Attorney Joseph Kelly's office is and Bargain Furniture. This would have been in the late 40's to middle 50's.

Mr. Borden was born in New York State in 1801. He died in

Borden, Texas, in 1874, but his body was taken to New York City for burial.

In 1822 he was headed for New Orleans but apparently, like the rest of us, he recognized the beauty of Amite County and stopped here for seven years. He worked as the county surveyor, also as a teacher in Bates and Zion Hill. I don't know where Bates was. How about this? He was known not for walking, but for running to work.

He went to Texas during the revolution and was often just one step away from being caught by the Mexicans. He and others published the first newspaper there. The Mexicans finally caught up with him and he was arrested. They threw his printing press into Buffalo Bayou. But it was only days before the Texans won the war at San Jacinto so his imprisonment didn't last long.

He was involved in Texas politics and also plotted the towns of Houston and Galveston. One of his inventions, in 1848, was a sail-powered wagon designed to travel over land and the sea.

In 1849, Gail Borden Jr. invented a "meat biscuit", a preserved food that although not a financial success, gained recognition for him as an inventor. He went to England to receive an award in London. Returning to the U. S. by ship, many children became ill when they drank contaminated milk. Supposedly this motivated him to perfect the process of condensing milk.

Condensed milk was patented in 1856 after three years of sorting out the procedure, and admittedly that's a lot of years after he lived in Amite County.

Condensed milk wasn't an instant hit but became important during the Civil War. We proud Amite Countians who've bragged on Gail Borden Jr. for many years should be aware that he sold his condensed milk primary to the Union Army. There was such a demand that several plants were opened. This product was responsible for his financial success after a life of many ups and downs. Civil War veterans continued to want it after that conflict.

Read about Gail Borden Jr. and one thing you'll conclude: he wasn't a quitter. He just kept stubbornly after things until he succeeded. This is a very thumbnail sketch of his life. Perhaps you'll want to read more.

## TAKE FIVE

Five minutes isn't very long. How important can that little time be?

This morning, during an early walk, I was two streets over from my home. The neighboring street is strictly residential, and has a speed limit of 25 mph. There's a school bus stop, and three young mothers with a total of nine children were waiting for the bus, which wasn't in sight. Some of the children were on each side of the street.

From where the bus stops, there's a small hill to the west about 300 feet. Suddenly a white extended cab pickup, clean, new and neat looking but with big jacked up wheels, topped the hill doing an estimated 50 mph in the 25 mph speed limit section.

Estimated 50 mph? That's my estimate, and since I used to do that as part of my job – estimate speeds – it's pretty close, might even be a bit low. It was a young male's kind of pickup. I waited just a second to see his face as he streaked by, and saw her face instead. A young woman. I expected her to slow down. Didn't happen.

A mother herself? She lives just over the hill on that same street. I see the truck when I walk by her house. Running late, most likely. Probably got a husband and perhaps a child or two up, fed, off to school or work, and then was running late to get to work on time.

I've often read that a five minute change in someone's schedule can help prevent such rushing. Go to bed five minutes sooner, get up and get going five minutes earlier.

Compare that five minutes to the lifetime of anguish over killing a child…anguish for her and her family, the child's family…mothers, fathers, aunts, uncles, grandparents affected. Is the hurrying worth it? Certainly with hindsight, no. And as a law enforcement officer for more than 30 years, I saw it way too often.

At 50 mph, a reasonable estimate of her speed, from the precise time she topped the hill 300 feet away, if a child had darted into the roadway at that very moment and she'd been paying attention , it would have taken her 175 of those feet to think – react – brake and stop her truck.

The most important point for any driver to remember is that

if you double your speed – say from 25 mph to 50 mph – your braking distance does not become twice as long, it becomes FOUR times as long.

"Wow!" I remarked to one of the mothers as the errant driver whisked by. "Happens every day," she replied. And I agree, since I see it too. Where are we all going in such a hurry? A five minute sooner start could make a big difference for many. Please think about it.

## WEST NILE VIRUS

Returning to Amite County from out West last Saturday, I stopped at a gas station near Ft. Worth, Texas.

As I stood at the pumps, a youngish black man, probably in his mid-40s, pulled up next to me. He exited his specially-equipped van – it had hand controls – on a scooter for the mobility impaired. I asked him if he needed a hand.

"No, but thanks," he said. He remarked that the Veterans Administration had helped him acquire his special equipment and it was working well for him. It was obvious that his physical problems were mostly in his legs.

"Iraq or Afghanistan?" I asked, probably being a little too nosey. "Neither," he replied. "West Nile Virus." His answer surprised me.

We chatted. He and his wife – she had gone inside the store

– both did 20 years in the Air Force, as administrative types. It takes a lot of that kind of effort to send just one fighter or bomber off into the Wild Blue Yonder. They did much the same kind of work I did for about half the 28 years I was associated with the AF. We had much in common, and our conversation came easily.

Isn't that ironic? He and his wife gave a combined 40 years of their lives to the U. S. military around the world, then a darn mosquito bit him in our country and now he can't walk. His attitude seemed to be good, though. They were completing a 7,000 mile trip from Sacramento, California, to the East Coast and return, visiting relatives. One final stop had been planned in Las Vegas for a little fun.

But a family member had just passed away in California and they were skipping Sin City. "Just doesn't seem right," he remarked. "The mood back home is sad, and we wouldn't feel good going to a party town just before returning home for a funeral."

I finished refueling, as someone waited for me to move so they could gas up. My disabled short-time new friend didn't know it, but I said a little prayer asking the Good Lord to help him recover as we gave our special AF handshake "so long". "We're everywhere!" He said, smiling, referring to us ole blue suiter vets.

Thank God for the Veterans Administration which helps those who've given a substantial portion of their youth for our country's good, and sometimes have come up with a physical problem in the process, even something as unlikely as West Nile Virus. Of course we sometimes hear complaints, but the VA is one of the two government agencies I most often hear good things about. The other one is the Social Security Administration.

## BITS AND PIECES

My mind is in a swirl. Just bits and pieces are jumping into this column, this week. Sorry!

Dale Evans...we wrote about Dale a while back, and today's comments aren't the end of this story. Someone wrote from Texas that they claim Dale out there. Hey, nobody gets our Dale! Folks in McComb e-mailed that a friend over their way has more information, my apologies for not following up yet. It's been a LSTD kind of month. Lotta Stuff to Do.

Just noticed on the Internet that a sale of Dale's and Roy's things brought some pretty incredible prices. Sad that their era is mostly lost forever. You and I were born at the right time, the article says. We were able to grow up with these great people even if we never met them.

It was a great ride through childhood. I have one photo of my 10th birthday which I celebrated in the back yard of a little brick house across from the ice house in Liberty. I'm barefoot-ed, but proudly showing off my brand new set of Roy Rogers' sixguns. Cap guns, of course.

*Residence across from Ice House in Liberty, Mississippi, present day.*

At the sale, Dale's stuffed horse, Buttermilk, sold below the presale estimate of $30-40K, for $25,000. But her parade saddle, expected to bring between $20-30K, brought in $104,500! Trigger, Roy's horse, sold for $266,500. Bullet, their dog and their real pet, went for $35,000, three times the presale estimate. Oh, those critters were stuffed.

Stay on that Happy Trail, Dale, we'll get back to you.

We've talked about the F-86 jet fighter on IH55, near Hazlehurst. Mr. Tom Lewis of Liberty Insurance Agency in Liberty remembers it being lifted into place in 1968 while he cruised up and down IH55 commuting to Mississippi State. He says there's either a former VFW or American Legion post building mostly covered up in the woods behind the aircraft, put in place as a display for whichever of the organizations was there. He helped me understand how to access the site and I'll be hopefully doing that soon, also. My appreciation to Mr. Lewis. Must talk my boss here at the WAR into a travel allowance!

Sad to see that comedian Phyllis Diller died recently. For several years my mother, Lucille Anders (Green) worked in the sewing department at Goudchaux's department store on Main Street in Baton Rouge. Among the many well-known persons she made clothes for was Mrs. Blanche Long, Governor Earl Long's wife. Another was Phyllis Diller.

I think Mrs. Long knew her and referred her to Goudchaux's and my mother's handiwork during a visit to Louisiana. I remember my mother saying that Ms. Diller was a real hoot, didn't quit cracking jokes the whole time. Her manager, Milton Suchin, was quoted as saying: "She died peacefully in her sleep with a smile on her face." I hope she was thinking of the nice dress that Lucille Anders crafted for her.

Why is my mind swirling? Just finished a 12 hour dash to Florida, where my wife waited for me to help with an unwelcome house guest, Tropical Storm/Hurricane Isaac. Got back at 5 am, tired but a safe trip. God is good. See you next week!

*Chapter 11*

———❧———

# BIBLE BELT STORIES

## CRUISING FOR COSCO TROUBLE

I'VE MADE MY wife mad. I've been making fun of her Cosco step-stool.

There are a few antiques in our home, and I like them. They're sentimental favorites. My great-grandmother's Singer pedal sewing machine, a Seth Thomas clock that sat on a mantle long ago, post office boxes from Peoria, Amite County - stuff like that.

Actually I'm an Amite County antique myself, and most days I like myself, though there are occasional exceptions.

Keep this quiet, please, but this Cosco step-stool is gonna have to grow on me.

It's the genuine 1950s article, although Cosco still makes new ones. Why, I can't imagine. They remind me of something that Lucille Ball might have yelled at Ricky Ricardo about. "WHERE IS MY COSCO STEP-STOOL, RICKY? DID YOU THROW IT OUT OF THE BIG TRAILER? FIND IT…NOW!!"

It arrived in original condition from eBay, looking as if hadn't had a cleaning since 1961, the year I graduated from high school. Funny that yellow is my favorite color, and yellow it is. The chrome legs and other parts were kind of rusty, but my wife's been scrubbing, and it's coming around.

I'm a fan of tank history, and this Cosco fits right in, reminding me of a Yugoslavian T-53 Hedge Row Flip Flopper, though I never figured on having one in the kitchen. The rust looked familiar.

The rascal has displaced my TV tray holder in the kitchen corner, and my tray stand was moved into a narrow space between the pedal sewing machine and the post office boxes. Where the Cosco should hide out, in my humble opinion.

Oh, wait a minute. Maybe I was wrong, for just the second time ever, the first being the one time I previously thought I was wrong. I need a safety stand to work on my three quarter ton pickup, something that'll support over 4,000 lbs. This ole Cosco T-53 step-stool may be just the ticket.

And the Cosco, too, has helped me revive another great Amite County growing-up tradition. Remember corn bread and milk meals? ONLY corn bread and milk? Suddenly my wife seems to be helping me enjoy those at night quite frequently, instead of doing her usual most excellent meal preparation. Told you the Cosco would be good for something!

*Cosco stepstool, oldie but goodie, 2017.*

Ever have a vague recollection of having seen a thing before? These step-stools have been made since 1941. I was born in 1943. Maybe there was one in Dr. Butler's clinic, in the hallway, between there and the Liberty Barber Shop, and opening my eyes to this world, maybe my first vision was of…well, just sayin' maybe.

Oops. My wife is calling me. What's that she's yelling? "HEY BUDDY, JUST KEEP IT UP AND THIS LITTLE STOOL IS GOING TO GROW ON YOU, ALL RIGHT. RIGHT OVER YOUR HEAD."

Gotta go now and clean out the bird cage. I'll be using the Wilk-Amite Record in the bottom. The same one, coincidentally, with this story. What a shame my wife will miss reading it.

## AWAY FROM HOME AT CHRISTMAS

How many veterans have spent one or more Christmases away from home? It's a lonely time, if one wishes to be with family and cannot.

In spite of 28 years military service, I was completely dispossessed of "home for the holidays" just twice, where there was no chance of getting there or spending some time with family. During the first, at age 24, I was in Thailand during the Vietnam War.

It was a long Christmas morning. At noon, the chow hall served a great turkey dinner, and a dessert that I'd never eaten. Bread pudding. A friend from New Orleans suggested I try it to lift my spirits. I did, it was good, and it did. Since then I have a special place in my heart for bread pudding.

Imagine being an American soldier and spending five straight Christmases away, even from fellow soldiers. Such is the case with Army Sgt Bowe Bergdahl, America's only known living war captive. He was captured in Afghanistan by the Taliban on June 30, 2009. In December 2011, perhaps thinking of home, he escaped, but was recaptured after three days.

His family lives in Hailey, Idaho. They want him back. The Taliban has released videos showing him in captivity. They're using him for a bargaining chip.

It's that time of year when we mail our Christmas cards. Rolling Thunder, an organization that supports veterans issues, wants a million cards sent to the White House to make the occupants aware there's an American POW who's been held for four and one half years, who's about to be away for home for his fifth Christmas.

If every effort can be expended to kill Bin Laden, can't the same effort be made to secure the release of a young American soldier?

Rolling Thunder would also like a million cards sent to Bowe directly through the Red Cross.

He could be your brother or your son or your grandson. Don't you have a few minutes, two extra Christmas cards and two extra stamps?

Mail Christmas cards to: U. S. Army Sgt Bowe Bergdahl, C/O The White House, 1600 Pennsylvania Ave. N. W., Washington, D. C. 20500.

And mail Christmas cards to: U. S. Army Sgt Bowe Bergdahl, C/O American Red Cross, 2025 E. Street, NW, Washington, D. C. 20006.

Are you into computers? Learn more about U. S. Army Sgt Bowe Bergdahl on Facebook at Bring Bowe Bergdahl Home.

Signatures are also being collected on a letter addressed to Secretary of State John Kerry, urging him to do everything possible to bring this soldier home. You can print the letter from The Grapevine web site at www.veteransgrapevine.com. Scroll down until you see a flying American flag and the words: Bring Home America's Only Known Living Prisoner of War. Click on it and follow the links.

I especially appeal to fellow veterans to help. Remember how you felt on Christmas? He's one of us. I know I can count on you.

(Author's note, 2017: As more information developed, it turned out that Sgt Bergdahl's conduct in Afghanistan was very questionable. Many veterans complained about the attention given him when he eventually returned home. I wrote this story before I was aware of all the information. That sometimes happens. My apologies.)

## TIME TO USE TIME WISELY

Ms. Essie Veal wrote effectively about the use of time in the November 22nd issue of the Wilk-Amite Record. She made me think about that.

As a child growing up in Amite County, I was taught to make good use of time, to work hard. My father was a hard worker who got up very early, 4:30 am. As a teenager, sometimes I was just coming in when he was already up. He'd just look at me, shake his head. It was a look that said: "You can't soar with the eagles if you're out running with the turkeys."

Over time, I realized the early bird does get the worm. There was always a worker who consistently arrived earliest, who gained an advantage over others who came dragging in later. A good friend for 40 years always told me: "We're burning daylight!"

Those who tried to be perfect often were outdone by others who moved along more purposefully, who did the important things well enough but not perfectly. The turtle's enduring pace did often eclipse the rabbit who dashed along helter-skelter.

I learned that making mistakes isn't always bad because the times we mess up are the things we really remember and normally don't foul up again. Once I read that experience is the sum of everything you've done wrong. Yes, there are good experiences, but the most meaningful are often those we goofed up on.

Ms. Veal detailed how one might add hours of achievement over those normally worked in order to achieve a dream. Absolutely true. Time wasted doesn't get us many places. Well, maybe the poorhouse.

It helped me to find a friend with a common dream and work together to achieve it individually. Example: Earning a master's degree. An Air Force buddy encouraged me to join him in that quest so we went to night school together. Without his encouragement - prodding even? - I may never have gotten started.

In my police career, the competition for promotions was very intense. It was a mistake to underestimate the time competitors would spend in preparation. Many took three months' vacation to study full time. The most I ever gave up was one month. The goal was to achieve a better income and a better life for my family. But that had to be balanced against giving up vacation time down the road.

So I decided early on that if I'd give up an eight hour day for such a purpose, I could only do it in good conscience by getting more than eight hours benefit. Thus my study schedule went from 8am until noon, 1:30 pm through 5:30 pm, then 7 pm until midnight, 7 days a week. I made up a six day schedule. The seventh day was used either to catch up when unexpected things interfered, or to get ahead. Daily, that was 13 hours of study, or a five hour gain over the eight hour vacation day I'd sacrificed.

Later in life, after careers were well in hand, I purposely devoted more time to my family and give up much of the ladder-climbing. My daughter was born when I was 40 and I gave more time to her than I had to my three sons. I never regretted it, though sometimes I wish I'd started sooner. In my Grandmother Anders' words, I finally learned to take time to smell the roses.

Thanks, Ms. Veal, for your reminders about time. I appreciate your take on things, a take that always has the Good Lord included.

Don't put this off. Do it now.


## LESSONS FROM THE BIBLE BELT

Merry Christmas! You're lucky if you're living in Southwest Mississippi and having a God and country inspired celebration. If you need a belt for your holiday dress or coveralls, a Bible Belt is best.

It's a time I think about my upbringing in Amite County. My father was an only child. His parents and his unmarried aunt and uncle lived together on the Gillsburg road. My sister and I were the only grandchildren. So we really had a double helping of grandparents in one house.

They didn't decorate or put up a tree unless I got one for them. There was a family heirloom, a marble-topped table, in their living room. As a young boy, my gift to them was going to the woods and finding a small tree for the top of that old table. And helping my great aunt, Myrtis Robinson, decorate it.

A buffet was in the dining room. The upper left hand drawer belonged to me. It had my toys, tools and other collectibles. During Christmas, that sideboard, decorated, was an integral part of the home and the holiday.

Sure, we gave and got presents. But church activities were central to Christmas and one was reminded it was the Christ-child's birthday. In my case the church was Liberty Baptist.

My dad and mother were hard workers. At other times, my father had a truck to repair or sawmill to get ready for the week's cutting. Weekend days that had the feel of Christmas Eve or Day weren't exempt from toil. But those days were.

I always had my family around, and the concept of family was deeply ingrained. I miss my parents and grandparents but am lucky to now have my own children, grandchildren and others. Regrettably, we're spread from Virginia to Arizona. More live in Texas than anyplace else. This last week, my wife and I spent a week in San Antonio, my adopted home for 28 years.

If you can ever get there and see the beautiful downtown Riverwalk, especially during Christmas, do so. The lights are dazzling. I spent 23 years as a police officer in San Antonio, the nation's seventh largest city. Two of those years were as the supervisor of officers around the Alamo. It's a bit odd to go as a tourist and celebrate Christmas where I used to chase crooks. But those days are behind me and now I chase my grandkids in the same place, in a different way.

Most of the artifacts of my Christmas past in Amite County

are gone, of course. But one survives. The old buffet from my grandparents' dining room was always dressed up for holiday meals. My mother and father inherited it, and had it professionally refinished. When they passed on, it was given to my niece in Dallas. My sister and I appreciate that someone younger in our family has it to cherish for many years.

*Author's sister, Faye Carol Hall, with their childhood buffet, 2015.*

My niece just sent me a photo of that old piece of furniture, decorated for the holidays, still an integral part of a family Christmas. I hope each of you has such a treasured item that survives. The memories they leave behind are wonderful. But it's great to see that old sideboard as a part of memories in the growing stage. Just remember, though, Niece Debbie, the upper left hand drawer is mine! Don't mess with my stuff.

May God bless each of you as we celebrate the birth of Jesus, His son, the Savior of the world.

*Chapter 12*

# DRAWING A LINE IN THE SAND

## REMEMBER THE ALAMO,
## AND THE MISSISSIPPIANS!

DURING A RECENT Christmas visit to San Antonio, Texas, my wife and I were privileged again to tour the Alamo. It's a special place, the Cradle of Texas Liberty. On March 6, 1836, 189 defenders were all killed by a Mexican army with more than 1,800 soldiers. Six hundred of the Mexicans died.

Many of you know that Jim Bowie, who spent a lot of time in this area, lost his life there. He was originally from Kentucky. Davey Crockett was killed there too. When Crockett, born in Tennessee, ran for a Congressional seat in that state in 1835, he declared that if he lost, the people in his district "may go to hell and I will go to Texas." Crockett lost the election and went to Texas, to die less than a year later. Forty-one defenders were born in Europe.

Do you know that some of the Texian soldiers were from Mississippi? Inside the chapel, there's a list of them by state birthplace. There were four.

Who were they, and what is known of them? Isaac Millsaps was the oldest at 41, having been born in 1795. He was a resident of Gonzales, Texas, was married, and had seven children. Where he was born in Mississippi or when he got to Gonzales isn't known. His wife, Mary, was blind. She was from Pike County. Millsaps had enlisted in the Gonzales Mounted Rangers on February 23rd, a unit formed to ride to the defense of the Alamo, and arrived on March 1st. He and the 31 other rangers in his unit are known as The Immortal 32. They rode in, knowing almost certainly they wouldn't ride out.

Willis Moore was also from Mississippi. Where isn't clear. Born in 1808, he was 28. He had been a member of the New Orleans Greys, a military unit that had arrived to join up with the Texians. The Greys were a much more polished and professional group of soldiers than the frontiersmen. Moore may have ridden in with Jim Bowie.

George Pagan, another Mississippian, was 26, having been born in 1810. One source says he'd been a resident of Natchez, another reports he was a native of that city. It's possible he was originally from Scotland. He was an artilleryman.

Christopher Parker, the youngest Mississippian at 22, had a distinguished lineage as a soldier. His grandfather fought at Valley Forge. His father was a soldier in the Battle of New Orleans in 1814. It's believed he arrived with a Captain Dimmett of Kentucky. Captain Dimmett had left the Alamo in February on a recruiting trip, but was captured by General Santa Anna's forces. About to be executed, Dimmett committed suicide before the Mexicans could kill him.

Any descendant of these Mississippi men who gave their lives for Texas freedom is a welcome member of the Sons or Daughters of the Republic of Texas.

If you're gonna mess around some place, don't do it at the Alamo. On February 19, 1982, British rock star Ozzy Osbourne urinated on the Centopath, the 60 foot tall memorial erected in 1939 to memorialize the defenders. There was a state-wide uproar. Osbourne was arrested and spent the night in jail. By public demand, he was banned from the state, and didn't return for 10 years until after he apologized for his immature behavior. The $10,000 he donated towards upkeep of the old mission probably helped.

Over 2.5 million people visit the shrine annually, and every Texan who's ever yelled: "Remember the Alamo!" honors courageous Mississippians Isaac Millsaps, Willis Moore, George Pagan, and Christopher Parker, heroes to this day.

*Captain Billy Anders, San Antonio TX Police Department,*
*on his retirement, at the Alamo, 1996.*

## THANK YOU FOR YOUR LIFE'S WORK

Mrs. Gladys Bell passed away January 15, 2012. Her obituary in the Wilk-Amite Record said she was a teacher for 43 years. I recall Mrs. Bell at Liberty Elementary School, although she was probably lucky not to have taught me.

I made good grades, but did it with disruption. I was a cut up, a comedian. Ha Ha! I added to most everything, and now realize I interfered with the efforts of good people like Mrs. Bell. Well, I guess that's why teachers get the big bucks, right? Ha Ha!

Her passing made me think about Liberty teachers who bravely gave me a jump start, when they should have been giving me a kick in the butt. I attended school in Liberty through the 6th grade before leaving for Oregon. Ha Ha! Said the relieved teachers.

Our school building then was in what is now Blaylock's Grocery. I recall a favorite memory or two of each grade.

*Formerly Liberty, Mississipi, Elementary School, now Blaylock's Food Center.*

In 1st, Mrs. Adams drew her infamous Coffee Pot on the blackboard. "Who had coffee this morning?" she'd glare, not wanting to see a hand. But Billy Causey would raise his, and I was jealous, so sometimes I'd raise mine too. I hadn't had any coffee, and my mother would have knocked me silly if she had seen my name in the Coffee Pot. But I wanted Dick, Jane and their dog Spot to admire me.

Mrs. Burdette suffered with me in 2nd grade. She was a cousin, and my mother threatened more mayhem on me if I called her

Cousin Lottie. "If you do and you make good grades, nobody will believe you earned them if your cousin is your teacher," my mother cautioned. She knew well the perils of small town living. But Cuddin' Lottie, oops, I mean Mrs. Burdette, kept some toys - plastic horses - on a table, and the first boy and girl who finished their work got to play with the toys. And horsing around was right up my alley.

Miss Anderson taught 3rd grade. We watched a film, with red arrows coming across the horizon, depicting the spread of communism. But I escaped from the commies in a car that also doubled as a boat, featured in My Weekly Reader. Everyone was going to have one, it said, either that or a car that doubled as an airplane. Hey, whatever happened to mine?

Mrs. Burris, 4th grade, the no-nonsense type, and I, the non-sense type, clashed, especially when she intercepted my love note to Patsy Sharp. Ouch. We Back Row Boys had to put our heads down with eyes closed at days' end and literally hear her drop a hat pin way up front, then raise our hands simultaneously, in order to leave to torture bus drivers. Of course we peeked, and were so well choreographed in hand-raising, we were smoother then than the LSU Golden Girls are now.

Poor Mrs. Melton, 5th grade. New swivel-type desks arrived, and one could spin round and round. I developed a daring little game of placing my pencil eraser against the metal part of the desk, swiveling at high speed, and seeing how close I could get the sharp pointed end to skid by my leg. Hey, I had the curse of the "A" name, we sat alphabetically, and I was isolated from my buddies. Someday, maybe (I said maybe) I'll show you the two tattoo-like dark dots that I still have above my right knee. Lead poisoning probably does strange things, and that could be my excuse even now.

Linda Robertson, now Carruth, says I wrote in her annual that year, 1954: "Roses are red, violets are blue, dandelions are small, and so are you. Ha Ha!" Well, wasn't I a charmer? Most likely my charm had something to do with why Linda's last name wisely became Carruth, and not..., well you get it.

Mrs. Gordon accepted the teaching challenge in 6th grade. Watching Durwood Brady's frantic dash to projectile vomit out the window after he swallowed some Red Man juice stands out as an academic highlight. And yes, there was that good will towards me when everyone learned I was leaving for Oregon. Never knew they liked me that much. Ha Ha. Bon voyage, dude!

After causing other teachers to rethink their career choice out West for two years, I returned to Liberty briefly in the 9th grade, actually attended class downstairs in the Little Red Schoolhouse before being permanently banished to Baton Rouge. It took more than 50 years to get Back Home but again you're stuck with me. Sorry. Ha Ha!

My sincere thanks to Mrs. Bell and others for their life's work in putting up with students like me. They are much appreciated!

## CALIFORNIA HERE IT COMES

Growing up in Amite County, one had a pretty good idea who was trustworthy and who wasn't. We picked our friends with that being one of the primary criteria. Who did you have faith in?

We knew our neighbors. Many people were on telephone "party lines". Listening to the conversations of others was often standard procedure. Each family had a distinct ring.

Your handshake meant something. Not too many people had to have something in writing. Of course, if a deal went bad, those same hands that shook on the sale/purchase might turn into fists, and the aftermath might be a fistfight. And the cops usually weren't called, especially if the offending party knew he'd done a bad thing.

The deadbeats, and yes, there were a few, were pretty well identified ahead of time.

Our socializing was done face to face, not on social electronic media as now. Driving around the county, I still remember places where my church had an all-day Saturday picnic, with softball and other games. One place is on Highway 48, out of Liberty towards Centreville, a field next to the West Fork of the Amite River.

Fast forward to today. I'm currently involved in a sale of an antique travel trailer, a 1952 Spartan Royal Spartanette, 35 feet long. It's not a tremendous amount of money, less than $6000.

Although in decent shape for its age, it needs restoration. But my buyer is in Los Angeles, California, and he's a movie producer and actor.

*1952 Spartanette travel trailer.*

This is a family newspaper and I won't even describe his word definition of "trust". Let's just say it doesn't start with a "T" and it's four letters long. One of the movies he was involved in during past years is titled: "I Spit On Your Grave." That should give you a hint. The ole Spartan may well wind up being used in a "slasher" movie for all I know.

It's been an interesting sales experience. Although he seems like a nice fellow - he's 50 in a few days - it's not a 1950s Amite County deal. His father is a lawyer and is used to the Hollywood scene, and has called the shots on that end. I have a 12 year plus 100% positive feedback history on several hundred transactions on eBay, the internet site where I sold this trailer. It doesn't seem to matter.

I've already provided more information to satisfy those skeptical California customers than I want to, and my Amite County stubbornness kicked in early this morning. I woke up thinking about it at 4 AM, so got up and sent them an offer to refund their deposit, though I don't have to, if we don't consummate this deal soon.

Whether I sell it or not isn't that important. It's just my self-imposed effort to downsize. I have no expensive toys but have too many cheap ones. And I bought the trailer to refurbish for use as a vacation home. It won't make me or break me one way or the other.

If it was 1955, and I was standing in front of the ice house in Liberty, it'd be about time to ball up my fist, and get it on. But we don't live like that anymore, do we? What a shame that sometimes is.

## THE OLE GRAY MARE

There probably was a time before the use of motor vehicles when a gray mare pulled some kind of wagon used by the U. S. Postal Service. If so, we know something that's true.

The ole gray mare, she ain't what she used to be.

The Post Office recently announced that Saturday mail delivery to homes and businesses would cease in August. Honestly, I've thought for a long time that would be a logical way to cut costs. I won't mind getting bills on Monday that might have come on Saturday.

The Post Office says the elimination of Saturday delivery will save $2 Billion a year. That means that current losses will drop to just $13 Billion a year, instead of $15 Billion.

There are universal truths. One is...you can't really go home again. Another, and it's closely related...the only thing constant in life is change. And how the Post Office has changed across the years. One noticeable thing, of course, is the price of stamps.

From 1932 to 1958, a first-class stamp cost 3 cents. After 1958, a steady increase in stamp prices took place, until it reached 46 cents this past January 27$^{th}$. You can bet it won't be long before a stamp is 50 cents.

Growing up in Liberty, I remember trips to the post office, located then next to Jimmy Sharp's appliance store. "Go get me a stamp," my mother would say, giving me a nickel, and expecting change. While there, I'd look at the posted pictures of the FBI's Ten Most Wanted. Was my mug shot up there, I'd wonder? Luckily, it never was. When the pictures changed, I was always curious. Did they get 'em Dead or Alive?

If you lived in the country, remember waiting for the mailman? You were on a RFD route. Rural Free Delivery. Is that term still used? Everyone anticipated the arrival of the Wilk-Amite Record or the Southern Herald, the Social Security check, or that little item you'd ordered from The Progressive Farmer.

The people working at the Liberty post office seemed to stay there for years, often their whole career. Now, probably due to union seniority rules, postmasters to come to work with a little red bandana tied on a stick, his or her personal belongings enclosed, ready to move at a moment's notice.

The Post Office says it will continue to deliver packages on Saturday, since so many of us order things on-line. Package delivery continues to increase, while the number of letters and cards keeps declining.

The Top Ten Most Wanted photos have been replaced, apparently, by the Top Ten Most Wanted Tax Forms. As the number of working people, and thus the number of taxpayers, continues to decrease, and the amount of money needed by the government increases, don't be surprised if you see a new poster soon that says: "Wanted, Taxpayers! Dead or Alive!"

The ole gray mare is straining at the bit.


## COMMON SENSE GOVERNMENT, FINALLY

There was a time when I thought my grandfathers and my father who lived in Amite County knew more than they did. They said that hard work was the key to success, and the way to achieve my dreams. They sure fooled me.

For 50 years I followed their advice and while I suppose working all that time earned me a retirement, there are other things I'd like to have accomplished. My passions, so to speak.

I'm a respectful U. S. citizen and I pay serious attention to our government leaders. Last week the White House was quoted as saying that Obamacare might actually lead to more unemployment since some might choose not to work or earn more since they could would be entitled to fewer health benefits as a result.

But, it was stated, that wasn't all bad, since those same folks would have time to live their passions.

Well, there you go. I've always been passionate about wanting to speak a couple of foreign languages, play the guitar and piano, and travel around the world. The travel may have had to be on a tramp steamer instead of a luxury cruise ship, but what the heck. It would have been the same world.

Doggone it. Had I been just a little lazier, and not have tried to advance through hard work and earn a better living for my family, maybe I'd have had time to do those things.

Actually, had I not had the stress of working, and the worry about paying my bills on time, perhaps my health would have been better and I'd have been less of a drain on the medical system, thereby conserving some of those health dollars for those who need them more. That would have proved me a compassionate person, wouldn't it? And if you take the "com" away from "compassionate", look what's left. Passionate. The way one has to act to achieve one's passions.

The White House has made it so much easier for me to understand than did my hard-working ancestors, whose bad advice has caused me to forego achievement of my passions.

But I'm learning all this a bit too late. Why didn't I know this when my dad handed me a wire brush and told me to remove all the rust from something the size of the Brooklyn Bridge, so that he could paint it? Or when I was helping my grandpa pick cotton? That was hard work, and I could have foregone that and have been achieving my passions instead. When I was a youngster, one of my passions was fishing.

I've learned way too late that my dad or granddad would have understood if I'd said I was passionate about going fishing, for example, on the same day they wanted me to help, and wouldn't have objected to my sitting under a shade tree and watching a bobber while they did that stupid menial work in order to earn a living. Heck, maybe they'd even have cleaned the fish if I'd caught anything, since to do so myself would have interfered with another of my passions back then, daydreaming.

Thank goodness we finally have people at the head of government with some common sense.

# Chapter 13

# PRAISE THE LORD AND
# PASS THE BULLETS

## IT'S ALL A GAS

IN THE 1950s, as a young Mississippi teenage driver, it was tough digging out $1.50 for five gallons of gas. I had little money so even a buck fifty seemed high. "Give me a dollar's worth," I often said.

What's the least you ever paid? In Arizona in 1968 during a gas war, I filled up for 16.9 cents a gallon, my personal low. My car held just 10 gallons. Can you imagine filling up now for $1.69?

The 30 cents a gallon we paid in 1957, adjusted for inflation, would amount to 96 cents a gallon today. Someone has been doing some serious adjusting since then, as gasoline is presently averaging $3.57 a gallon in Mississippi.

In 1955, I could see the gasoline I was buying at Mrs. Morgan's store, about three miles out of Liberty, just off the Gillsburg Road. The pump had a glass container on top. Gas was kind of like wine back then, where you could see it, almost touch it, sniff it, see it swirl it around before you consumed it.

That glass top gave you a chance to see a lizard or anything else floating around in there, something that might lodge in the carburetor. Something that would get in the way of my foot which was often in the carburetor.

Not sure why I said a lizard, but that reminds me of something else. My cousin George Rice and I were riding in the back of his dad's pickup, headed to Baton Rouge from Centreville. His father stopped in Slaughter for gas and George and I bought Royal Crown Colas. Glugging his down, Cousin George was startled to see a lizard in his soda pop bottle, the unfortunate critter apparently having been taking a siesta at the bottling plant.

So did we call a lawyer, sue somebody? Heck, we thought it was funny. Since George wound up making All-American at LSU and then playing professional football for five years for the old Houston Oilers, I think the lizard may have contained some growth hormones that were good for him. Good for Cousin George, not the lizard.

*LSU Defensive Tackle George Rice, All American,*
*1965, born Liberty, Mississippi.*

When I saw George's paychecks, I looked for another RC with
a lizard but couldn't find one.

Back to today and gas prices. I'm amazed that gasoline companies seem to delight in $4.00 a gallon fuel. When it's selling for
$2.00 a gallon or so, I look for excuses to hit the road. At $4.00
a gallon, I start walking to the store, and shut down except for

necessary travel. Wouldn't they do better by keeping the prices lower, and selling more?

Here's an example. Traveling fairly often between Florida and New Mexico by way of Mississippi, I pay attention to how many motor homes are on Interstate 10 during the 1,700 mile trip. When gas is around $4.00 a gallon, I've seen as few as half a dozen over three days. At that cost, people just park 'em.

The cost of gasoline is trending up now, and is predicted to do so through April. The American Automobile Association attributes rising prices to refinery issues, the price of crude oil, and economic optimism, which they say spurs investment in oil as a commodity, driving up crude oil's cost. The AAA says there's no good news when it comes to gas prices in the near term.

So maybe you'd better hop over to the store and fill up the old jalopy now, instead of later. If the gas pump hiccups, don't worry. It's probably just a lizard who was taking a nap at the refinery.


## WELDING THAT WILL HOLD

A young man was standing in front of me the other day in a restaurant as I waited to pay. He was ordering food to go. From the manner of his work clothes, I could guess he was a welder.

I spoke to him. He was 20 years old, and worked at a shop next door welding some sort of casing pipe. He was one of the most pleasant young men I've met in a long time. "Yes sir…no, sir," he said as we talked. Someone has taught him not only how to weld, but to have good manners.

Welders wear clothing that covers them completely, including a cap that will cover most of their head and neck. They protect themselves from hot sparks. My dad did a lot of welding at Anders Machine Shop in Liberty when I was a young boy, and I watched plenty of welding activity.

I didn't watch the "light" from the welding rod directly, of course. The warnings I got early on against doing that were similar to warnings about using a BB gun. "You'll put your eyes out!"

My dad was an expert welder. Good welders take pride in their work, and it's not easy to learn to do it quickly. Practice and experience are important.

A friend of mine in Texas was a beginning welder. My lawn-mower blade had broken, and he welded it together. His work looked good, but just in case, we picked our feet up safely when starting the mower. The welded end of the blade launched it-self about 50 feet to the side. "Back to the drawing boards," we laughed, retrieving the piece that went flying, using all our feet that luckily we still had.

I asked my dad once to fix an exhaust system on my car. He welded a new one from stainless steel, and it was well made. That car may not still be running, but someplace, somewhere, that exhaust system may still be around, if only in a heap of scrap metal.

My dad built a machine to automatically weld new surfaces on Caterpillar rollers, the part on which the tracks were affixed. My sister went to college on those rollers. When I'd see that machine running, the sparks flying, I knew my sister had called home. But she wouldn't have said: "Daddy, I need money." She would have told him: "Daddy, we need some more new rollers."

*George Davis (in his welding clothes) and*
*Lucille Anders at their Amite County farm, 1974.*

It was family code for the same thing, but it sounded better.

My father took pride in his work, and in doing good work for others. My sister and I and our children, his grandchildren, remember his excellent workmanship, and the example he gave us of working hard, in good fashion.

The young man I met the other day is probably still single, doesn't have a family. I didn't ask. But I hope that he and others like him continue to take pride in what they do, that they assemble things in a way that will last, and that their children and grandchildren, when they have them, will remember their craftsmanship.

He quickly impressed me as someone who would work in that manner, and I hope he will, because America needs quality workmen.

## LSU VS. IOWA

When a student at LSU, I lived in the bottom level of Tiger Stadium. It was the cheapest dorm on campus. I've mentioned before that my roommates and I lived within sight of Mike the Tiger's cage. We were always so broke, we tried to figure out ways to abscond with some of the meat he was fed. Mike lived pretty well.

Attending LSU games was a real treat. But I worked part-time away from school and could only get to about half of the home contests. Just once or twice in all the years since I graduated have I been back to Tiger Stadium to watch LSU play. It's something I've missed.

In 2005 I was out west during the Capital One Bowl in Orlando, Florida, when LSU played Iowa. Among the group of a dozen or so watching on television was a diehard Iowa fan. I was the only serious LSU supporter. LSU was ahead and was going to win. With just a couple of seconds left, Iowa only had a last second gasp and threw a Hail Mary desperation pass to the end zone on the final play.

You may remember the result. An Iowa player caught the ball and the Hawkeyes won. My friend ragged on me pretty hard and it's a little thing that's always been out there. One thing I know, though, is what goes around comes around, even though we sometimes have to wait a long time. Nine years in this case.

So when the Outback Bowl was set for Tampa, Florida, this past January 1ˢᵗ, and LSU-Iowa were the teams selected, I thought of my friend. I didn't call him but as Justin Wilson used to say, I "guar-un-tee" you he thought of me.

My wife and I called ole LSU friends who live nearby, and six former Tigers and Tigerettes, I suppose, drove to Tampa to watch the game. The ticket prices reminded me of one good reason I haven't seen many games since I was a student, but it seemed a rare opportunity.

It was cool and rainy, a real nasty day for the Tampa Bay area which sits smack dab in the middle of the land of sunshine. We bundled up in ponchos and took some sandwiches and had our own small version of a tailgate party. As rain dripped off my head, I wondered: "Are we really doing this?" A LSU loss would have convinced me of the foolishness of it all.

You probably know the outcome. The game wasn't pretty with our big-name quarterback out of action, and a freshman QB subbing. But the Tigers got it done, 21-14. Thinking back to 2005 as we walked back to the car, my ears were burning. Someone out west was thinking of me, and his ears were burning too. And no, I haven't called him, it would be pointless.

I know he knows, and he knows I know he knows, and I'll let it go at that. He knows I could call him any day and say: "Hey, how about them Tigers?" Think I'll save it for when I really need it.

My congratulations to Ole Miss and Mississippi State fans as well. When push came to shove, all our teams pushed pretty well, didn't they?

## WHERE ARE THE BULLETS?

It's really mostly your fault, ladies.

In the "old days", if we wanted ammunition, we went to the hardware store and got it. Seldom was there a problem finding what we needed. Every little grocery store carried a few boxes of .22 rounds.

All that changed for the worse, perhaps beginning around 2006. What happened? Is it something our federal government has done, the one many of us don't trust?

The January 2014 issue of NRA magazine, American Rifleman, has some explanations. I trust the NRA's explanation more than if the feds were telling the story. The writer is Frank Miniter.

Here's a summary. Demand has outpaced supply. The information on which to base this report came from manufacturers like Federal, Winchester and Remington. Excise tax collection figures were also used.

Excise tax brought in from ammo purchases began climbing after 2006 when gun sales began surging. The demand for ammunition doubled over five years. Ammo manufacturers have had a hard time keeping up. It takes investment in costly machinery and more production people. Companies are reluctant to invest in such expensive resources until they believe increased demand is a permanent change.

Have federal government purchases cornered the market? The Department of Homeland Security includes 70,000 plus law enforcers and more than 40,000 Coast Guard members, who must be supplied with ammunition, so DHS purchases large quantities. But even the makers of ammo say that government contracts, which actually reduced the number of rounds purchased from 2011 to 2012, are not responsible for the problems.

All agree it's "extremely high demand". All the major bullet makers, including Steve Hornady, president of Hornady Ammunition, say there is no government conspiracy.

Over 10 years from 2002 to 2011, there's been more than a 54% increase in background checks. Conceal-carry permits increased in number from less than a million in the mid-1980s to 6.8 million by the end of 2012.

And here's a biggie. More than five million women now are

active shooters. That figure has gone up more than 46% since 2001. This trend is still present, as the number of women gun owners keeps increasing.

Why are we so interested in firearms? Personally I believe it's a lack of confidence in our government to guarantee the safety of our citizens, but the NRA article doesn't address that issue, just the numbers. That's a whole 'nother story.

The ammunition crisis does seem to be lessening somewhat as ammo makers catch up with demand.

Praise the Lord and pass the bullets!

# Chapter 14

# FOOD FOR THOUGHT

## JOHNSON CREEK

**WHERE WAS YOUR** Johnson Creek?

My youngest son and his family were in Orlando, Florida, this past week. They were on a vacation to Disneyworld. He, his wife, and three children spent their 4th of July holiday in a way they'll long remember.

Their youngest child is four. She still believes in the Tooth Fairy, Santa Claus and Snow White. While traveling to Florida by airplane, she even wore her Snow White dress.

Growing up in Southwest Mississippi, my family and I rarely enjoyed the kind of vacation my son and his family took this past week. Money, of course, was a big factor. Our 4th of July outing was more likely a trip to the lake at Percy Quinn Park, or even a swimming outing to the Amite River at Peoria or to Bates Bridge.

My daughter, who lives in Texas, is stepmom to three children and mother to another one. My "little girl" is the youngest of my children by 10 years. So she and her husband are really just getting started in this marathon we call life. With four, she has the most kids of any of my children and the least money to vacation with.

Down the road from her home, just a couple of miles, is Johnson Creek. It's a little tributary of the Guadalupe River. There are small waterfalls and shallow water where the kids can play safely. A few years ago, I took my old yellow Ouachita canoe to their house and left it. It was my home on the water on many trips and I've paddled literally thousands of miles in it. Even though it's kind of beat up, to my grandson, Kaleb, it's a mighty boat.

My daughter was likely working on both sides of the holiday and probably on the holiday itself. But hopefully there was time for a couple hours trip to Johnson Creek with some sandwiches, soda pop, and maybe a watermelon. The old canoe probably went along. Johnson Creek is their swimming hole, and the Good Lord takes care of the chemicals needed to clean and maintain it, not to mention the water needed to fill it.

Years from now, both families will recall their family vacations.

But will my daughter and her family be worse off for having been able to only go a couple of miles to Johnson Creek? I doubt it.

I suspect her children will recall the days fondly, and regret that they're done with, when they are. They'll remember splashing and yelling and learning to swim and stopping for a while to eat and waiting for an hour to get back in the water and the snake they saw a couple of times, and having fun with their friends and shivering sometimes and drying off in the sun and saying: "Do we have to go home already?"

If you ever went to Disneyworld, do you remember that or your Johnson Creek kind of days better? I bet I know the answer. Here's hoping your 2013 July 4th celebration caused some things to stick in your head that won't shake loose for a long, long time.


## COOLING OFF

Good ole July. Hotter than baked beans at a BBQ. At this age, the heat gives me fits but I still get outside to work in it. These days, I try to schedule my projects within 50 feet of the garage, the length of my extension cord, so that my Blue Blower shop fan can keep me company.

I think back 60 years to being a boy in Southwest Mississippi. The summer heat was just part of life, and taken for granted. You just didn't know any different. Air conditioning? You've got to be kidding. The evening coolness on the porch, rocking slowly in the swing, was the first relief from the day's baking by the sun. At night, you were lucky to have a small fan.

Days out of school meant riding a bike to something with water in it. In Liberty, that required a trip through the cemetery to reach Tanyard Creek. We didn't swim there but did some serious playing.

My dad had the ice plant and often I was called upon to deliver a small block of ice to a house in town. I carried it in a basket on my bike, and "hurry hurry" was the order of the day, delivering ice out in the sun.

Today I drink water mixed with Gatorade to keep the ole engine turning. The two most refreshing things I remember drinking as a boy still linger in my mind. One was cool, fresh well water at my grandma's house. When the wooden bucket kept on the porch was almost empty, the honor system dictated that you refill it if you'd taken the last drink. The little bit at the bottom was tossed out onto the elephant ears, which were gigantic.

Everyone drank out of the same dipper, something we'd probably avoid today. I guess we thought that within families, we were all in the game together.

The other cold drinks I'll never forget were the soda pops at the ice plant. As you might guess, ice was plentiful and a big metal tank – maybe it was a #1 washtub, I've forgotten, although I remember something big and circular instead – held the coldest cold drinks in town. Back then, they were "cold drinks", not soda pop. My favorite was Dr. Pepper, and 10-2-4 has remained stuck in my mental vocabulary. Of course, we drank from glass bottles.

Today I wear athletic shoes to work outside, but I remember clearly the only naturally air conditioned part of me back then. My feet. I didn't wear out many shoes in the summertime of my youth. My soles must have been tougher then, because if I tried to walk very far now without footwear, there's only three words I could think of to say: Ouch, ouch, ouch!

A summer day in Mississippi 60 years ago might find me getting my fishing gear together, and heading for one of the three ponds on my grandpa's place, or even to a neighbor's pond. Such a fishing trip, if a friend was with me, might easily turn into a swim, seeking out the cool spots in the pond.

The ultimate way to cool off, though, was beyond biking or walking range and help was needed from my folks and their car. A trip to Percy Quinn Park or to the Amite River, with a watermelon cooled off in the water, was about the ultimate.

Some people might think we had it rough, growing up in the Mississippi countryside or a small town, but it seems to me God was pretty good to us.

*Amite River near Peoria, Mississippi, today.*
*The author learned to swim here in 1949.*

## WORKING TOGETHER

Together everyone achieves more.

Most of you probably paid attention to at least the outcome of the George Zimmerman murder trial completed last week in Florida. Maybe you were happy with the outcome. Maybe you weren't.

It's a tragedy whenever anyone loses their life, especially when the person is a teenager, someone young just getting underway. Trayvon Martin's death is no exception.

The burden of proof in a criminal trial is beyond a reasonable doubt. Any reasonable doubt. As a career law enforcement officer, I doubted that what I heard during the trial of Zimmerman's conduct could be proven to be criminal under that standard.

When Dr. Vincent Di Miao, the forensics expert, testified that Zimmerman's account of who was where during the confrontation was borne out by blood and other evidence, I was swayed that Zimmerman was probably being truthful although with all the attention, I was still uncertain how the trial would end.

Dr. De Miao was the county medical examiner in San Antonio, Texas, during my law enforcement career there and in my view, is indeed an expert. He's not a personal friend but I'm very familiar with his work.

We should remember, too, that Zimmerman wasn't proven innocent, but not guilty.

While reading the wrap-up of the Zimmerman trial, I saw a picture of a 12th grade AAU National girls basketball team that won second place in a July 4th national tournament. They didn't win the championship but were happy to have come in 2nd place, a fine achievement.

Their photo showed black girls and white girls smiling and embracing, holding up their V for Victory signs. Their team motto is just that: T.E.A.M., Together Everyone Achieves More. And they did.

In Gloster, Mississippi, and indeed all of Amite and Wilkinson Counties, we're all on the same team, so to speak. Like it or not, we're stuck with each other and need to make the best of it. Isn't what that AAU girls' basketball squad achieved an important lesson for us? Teamwork is important.

I wasn't riveted to the Zimmerman trial, but probably watched about three hours of it. The parents of Trayvon Martin caught my attention. In my opinion, they handled a very tough situation with style and grace. It's hard for me to imagine putting myself in their place.

If all of us can handle the outcome with the grace of Sybrina Fulton, Trayvon Martin's mother, we'll be okay. When the verdict was announced, she shared her favorite Bible verse with others: "Trust in the Lord with all your heart and lean not on your own understanding; in all your ways submit to Him, and He will make your paths straight."

Maybe all of it is even a good lesson for Gloster politics.


## STOPPING BY PEPITO'S

This past Sunday, I came back home through Gillsburg, hit all the bumps down Main Street in Liberty, unloaded and installed an electric dryer for my Aunt Marjorie between Liberty and Gloster (thanks, Charlie, for the help!), then went by the Wilk-Amite Record in Gloster.

Southwest Mississippi is very beautiful with all the recent rain.

The grass is growing lustily and the Amite River is full. In Gloster, I had Main Street all to myself. The rest of you were in church where I should have been.

I was headed west. Indeed, this is written from the mountains of southern New Mexico. Tomorrow I'll travel farther north to Chama, New Mexico, just a few miles from Colorado. My wife and I are working a two week volunteer assignment with the Cumbres & Toltec historical narrow gauge railroad which runs from Chama to Antonito, Colorado, at elevations up to 10,000 feet. We're members of its Friends Committee. She'll fly to Santa Fe this weekend. More on that venture next week.

I lived in San Antonio, Texas, for 28 years. For a Mississippi country boy who grew up on grits and fried chicken, I sure fell hard for Tex-Mex cooking. There are fantastic little mom and pop cafes scattered all about that country. Trips on Interstate 10 in West Texas take you through Ft. Stockton, a travel hub where many stop. I've visited there often and have accumulated enough Ft. Stockton stories to write a small book.

My daughter graduated from Sul Ross State University in Alpine, Texas, not far from Ft. Stockton, another past reason for my frequent visits.

With gasoline so costly, and pulling a small travel trailer, I travel on the cheap. It's tough to justify spending money on motel rooms when I'm already dragging a little bedroom. Thus I frequently stay overnight on Walmart parking lots, which they allow. Leaving the Ft. Stockton Walmart early this morning,

I headed for one of my favorite places in the world, Pepito's Café. The food there is as good as it gets.

Roy Urias is the owner. His restaurant is named for his grandson, Pepito. There's a mural painted on the wall with a picture of Pepito and Roy's Chihuahua, Senor Spud. The painting was done in 2002, when Mr. Urias opened his café. Though he's getting a little long in the tooth, Senor Spud is still with us.

Pepito's is a gathering place for locals and out-of-towners, too, who're familiar with its location on the east end of the old main street through Ft. Stockton. Roy's friends often call him Danny Boy. Pepito's has a drive-through window and many locals do just that. But I like to go in and sit down and check things out. Today was no exception.

I had a breakfast burrito, and it was so good, I had another breakfast burrito. Sorry, I was bad, just couldn't help myself. Ashley and Carla were the servers today, and it was kind of their fault, because they were friendly and Ashley asked me if I wanted another one after I had the first one. Wouldn't it have been impolite to say no? Carla kept me in coffee and ice water.

Like yesterday, when I drove through Amite County, today was a great day! Stopping at Pepito's and visiting with the good people there and eating their good food is one of my favorite things to do, and for sure one of the Good Lord's blessings.

Now if I can just get them to learn how to cook grits and fried chicken…

## COUSIN CAGELENE

This is not an obituary, just a tribute to a first cousin who was important to me.

Cagelene Rice Crawford was lucky as were many of us. She was born in Amite County, Mississippi. Her life took her other places, though, and except for a few relatives here, you have probably never heard of her.

She was close in age to my only sister, and I am close in age to her only brother. So as first cousins, the four of us knew each other quite well.

She grew up in Baton Rouge, a star majorette at Istrouma High School. She continued those activities in the LSU band. The living room in her parents' home at 3352 Ropollo Street was a museum-like place of her trophies. Later in life, she taught others like her daughter Dana and made their costumes. She was devoted to that interest, and without doubt was a positive influence in many a young girl's life.

My family moved to Baton Rouge in 1957. She and her brother were the only people in my age group that I knew. I lived near Plank Road but on the wrong side of it to attend the same school they did. In order to do so, my parents had me use their address. My mother drilled it into me…having me repeat if often…write it down a few hundred times.

"3352 Ropollo Street," I'd respond, when asked where my home was. I've never forgotten it. In reality I only spent a few nights. But I visited often, and Cagelene was always there.

She was sharp-witted, no one's dummy. She said what she thought. There was no doubt as to where she stood on an issue. Life, marriage and two children took her to Slidell, Louisiana, then to Ruston, between Shreveport and Vicksburg MS, on Interstate 20. I last visited her about five years ago. She'd been seriously ill, and I drove from Gloster up through central Louisiana, through the cotton fields of the delta.

I quietly repeated that same route on Saturday, October 17th, and it wasn't a day for listening to the radio, but for reflection on her and her life. Like many of us, she knew the adage: "All God's chillen have their troubles." She had hers. But she dealt with them courageously, and successfully.

It was obvious from those at Trinity United Methodist Church in Ruston that "Miss Cagelene" was well thought of. I was privileged to represent first cousins and make a few remarks. Mostly I talked about her youth since others present didn't know her then. I remember those gatherings of cousins at our Grandmother and Grandfather Rice's home which stood just immediately west of where the Amite School Center is now.

Cagelene was always a star attraction, and I can clearly visualize her baton as it as it flew high into the air, to be caught without hitting the ground. Sometimes it was on fire. Yes, she lit the ends with something, probably cigarette lighter fluid, and she always snagged it before it touched the earth! Amazing.

Though it never occurred to me then, her name is a bit unusual. I've never heard of another "Cagelene". Her grandfather's name on her mother's side was Cage, and her mother honored her own father by adding the last part. They were the Jacobs family of the Ford community, not far north of Liberty. Many older folks will remember the Pecan Grove out near their home.

Reta Cagelene Rice Crawford was 74, almost 75. She started life in Dr. Butler's clinic in Liberty, next door to the Liberty Barber Shop. I guess her folks had confidence in our physician, and drove up from Baton Rouge for the event.

Rest in peace, Cuz', you are remembered and appreciated!

*First cousin Cagelene Rice Crawford, born Amite County, Mississippi.*

## HISTORIC OLDE DOWNTOWN

Tuesday's election winners are unknown as this is written but I congratulate the victors and thank those who ran for office out of a sense of service. The jobs aren't easy.

Often, winning a political post results in "be careful what you wished for". Having held a couple, I remember wondering: What was I thinking? If you satisfy 51% of constituents, you've done well.

We'd like our politicians to help restore our downtowns to their former glory. We regret that the crowds gathered on our Main streets back in The Day aren't there now. Then, people were largely stuck in the country. Coming to town was a big deal. There was a variety of stores. Not many people could routinely drive 20 miles to a bigger place. You certainly wouldn't ride a wagon pulled by a mule team that far.

I recall going to Liberty with my grandpa on his wagon, and we only went two and one half miles. We'd tie up behind the M&T Store. To there and back home was an all day trip.

It was a big social thing, too. In Liberty, on a Saturday, my folks would shop but much of the afternoon and night was spent parked on Main Street, in front of what is now Reynolds Florist, visiting - watching others walk by - gossiping - whatever. Then, our Facebook time was live, face to face. Now social lives are more varied, transportation is easier, and most of us have more discretionary money, no matter how bad things may seem.

Isn't it time we gave up hope for downtown Gloster? Hey, relax. What I mean is the former reality of it. Things have changed, and we have to adjust. Recently I saw a sign in the downtown area of Prattville, Alabama, that read: "The town where perservation and progress go hand in hand." I think that's what I mean.

Downtowns still have a role, if not in the traditional way. Grant monies are available for "reshaping" downtowns visually into what we consider the old style. Many have been refurbished that way. Round globe lights mounted on poles have returned. The sidewalks, or a portion, have been bricked into checkerboard walkways.

Sylvester, Georgia, has a downtown that originally was much like that of Gloster or Liberty or Centreville. It's been refurbished in the new "old" style. The Chamber of Commerce director said monies for Sylvester's redesign came from federal grants. If you looked in the other direction from the downtown area, you'd have seen an antique car show in progress, where the old railroad tracks and depot were. It was Saturday and Sylvester was hopping! Prattville, Alabama, had a very similar good look.

Old downtowns typically have cheap unused buildings, good for such as arts/crafts stores, thrift stores, businesses like that.

At some point we have to throw in the towel and admit that "it ain't gonna be what it used to be", but it can be very attractive, very workable. Many cities now officially name their old downtowns the Historic Olde Downtown, and act accordingly.

Passing through Gloster, I wouldn't be much tempted to divert off Highway 24 in response to the sign with an arrow which points simply to "Downtown". I know what I'm likely to find.

But what if the sign said Historic Olde Downtown? My curiously would be aroused. I'd think: Just what are these brash folks doing that makes their downtown deserve that name? What of a historical nature can I see? I'd be tempted to look.

Food for thought, which just might be consumed, of course, at Gloster's new café in our own historic olde downtown.

*Chapter 15*

# EARNEST PRAYERS

**REMEMBERING MY DAD**

**FATHER'S DAY THOUGHTS,** a week early…

When our telephone rang back in 1982 and my wife answered it and I saw the expression on her face, I knew it wasn't a good call. It was my mother, telling us my father had passed away.

He'd been ill with cancer so it wasn't that big of a surprise, but any one extra day you can keep them around is a good thing.

Thirty years ago, how the time flies. He's buried at the Robinson Baptist Church cemetery at Peoria. At the grave site recently, I reflected on the many ways he helped me. He wasn't the touchy-feely type but he worked hard, supported us, and lived up to his responsibilities. He was honorable, his handshake meant something.

We'd moved to Baker, Louisiana, near Baton Rouge, for the purposes of his work. But he was Amite County through and through. During my upbringing he'd taught me a few of his skills. Eventually I made my living a whole different way, but I've changed out my share of motors and transmissions, and done more than a few brake jobs.

Speaking of transmissions, in a few minutes I'll change the oil and filter in the one in my Jeep since my shop doesn't want to. It has a minor modification, and they only like to do the easy, straight-forward jobs that produce the most money in the short-est time, with the least risk they'll mess something up. Honestly, I really don't want to get down on the garage floor and soak up the fluid, but I have my dad to thank for the knowledge that al-lows me to do it.

He had many practical, common-sense suggestions in his teach-ing. Here's one. When working on something and things are going south, get on the other side of it and look at that opposite side. You'll see it from a whole new angle and you'll see new ways to approach the job that will help you.

A quick example might be changing out a starter on a car. From the top, looking down, you see one thing. But crawling under-neath, looking up, you'll clearly see where the two bolts are that connect it to the engine block, especially the inside bolt. And you'll be able to get to them much easier from under the car.

If you're a person who's not into such things, the same advice can be applied to everyday life, and doing so has helped me. If you're older and more mature, you're probably learned this, most likely the hard way.

Two people each have their own version of a story or something that happened. Listening to one only, you might say: "Why, that rascal! What he did is really bad. I don't like that. He'll get his."

But what you really learn in life, especially as you gain experience, is this. There's two sides to every story. When you take time to first get the other side of what happened, the situation will probably take on a different tint. In other words, look before you leap. The truth of a matter is usually not at one extreme or the other, but somewhere in between.

So, just like changing out the starter, by looking at things from the opposite side before going for the wrench, you'll see things that will help you sort things out in a better way.

Thus my father's teachings stay with me, even if he's gone. This is one big reason it's good to stop and reflect on the things our dads did for us. So, Happy Father's Day, pa. I'll do the knuckle-banging for both of us this afternoon so you can rest in peace. I'm proud to be your son and I love you.

**THANK GOD FOR FATHERS**

Father's Day is Sunday, June 16th, and I'm thinking about my dad.

He passed away in 1982 and his earthly remains rest peacefully now in Amite County, in the Robinson Baptist Church cemetery in the community of Peoria. "Out towards McComb, north of Gillsburg," we might say, if we're looking eastward from Gloster or Liberty.

One of the things I remember about growing up here are Sunday afternoons. "Let's take a ride," my dad would beckon the family. Television was in its infancy. There were movies but there was no Netflix, movies were just shown in town. And not on Sundays, by the way. That was God's day.

Gasoline was perhaps 30 to 35 cents a gallon. That sounds cheap but my folks' income wasn't that much. I recall when my father began making $100 a week in the 1950s and we thought we'd really arrived!

From Liberty or close to it, we might venture out 20 or 30 miles on a Sunday afternoon ride in any direction, having gone to Liberty Baptist Church on Sunday morning…and needing to be back by 6 PM for Training Union.

Maybe the ride would include a swim at Bates Bridge on the West Fork, or at Peoria on the East Fork. If you're from Amite County, you don't need to be told the West Fork or the East Fork of what river. You already know.

My dad's youth was spent largely around Peoria. There was a time when Peoria was called Robinson. But when a post office was applied for, there was another Robinson in Mississippi which had existed even longer, so another name had to be found, thus Peoria. I don't know why.

*My father's childhood home in Peoria, Mississippi.*
*It burned in the early 1900s.*

In my home, I have the mail boxes that belonged to Peoria. My dad was paid to tear down the old post office building, which had fallen in, and he kept the boxes. My folks weren't especially proud of possessions but those boxes were an exception. They had them professionally framed and they still look good. We took them to Liberty and displayed them a few years ago during the Bi-Centennial.

There's even a little mystery involved with those mail boxes. There are 24 boxes but they're numbered from 121 to 148, that's 28 numbers. Four of the numbers are missing and I don't know why that is, either.

*Post office boxes from the 1960s used in Peoria, Mississippi.*

My dad may have known and it's too bad he isn't around to tell me. I wish I could ask him, and it would be great to give him a hug and wish him Happy Father's Day, too. He'd be 97 now.

As with most fathers and sons, we had our tough days, but I thank God for all my earthly dad did for me and meant to me.


## COUNTING BLESSINGS

Here's hoping your Father's Day was as good as mine. Some days are too perfect so I build in the 10% factor.

I reserve the right to downgrade even a fantastic day in advance. I've been around too long and know that even as late as midnight, something may punch a hole in my party balloon.

Anyway, yesterday was a 90% good day, for sure! Here were a few of my blessings.

My wife called from out West announcing her safe arrival. She and 11 other gals from her gym are hiking Bryce, Zion and Grand Canyons over the next week.

My long-time Baton Rouge buddy, Jerry Martinez, who lives in Ft Myers, Florida, invited me down so we could buy each other a Father's Day lunch. His wife is in North Dakota visiting family. Jerry and I went to Prescott Junior High, Istrouma High and LSU together. His dad worked at Esso. His mother, who just celebrated her 90th birthday, was my mother's friend during their similar careers in Baton Rouge as seamstresses. Mrs.

Martinez retired from J. C. Penney's at Delmont Village on Plank Road.

Jerry and I had a long delayed agreement to canoe the Orange River near his home. It's a beautiful little spring-fed waterway which flows into the Caloosahatchee River which in turn empties into the Gulf of Mexico. Over three hours, we paddled 12 miles and told war stories. Mine are mostly figments of my imagination.

But Jerry was an Air Force pilot during Vietnam and dodged bottle rockets which weren't 4th of July in nature during such events as the siege of Khe Sanh. There, he made combat assault landings in delivering supplies to our Marines, surrounded by more than 50,000 North Vietnamese soldiers. So his stories are mostly true. I emphasize mostly.

It was my first canoe outing since being involved in a nasty car wreck last October when my right shoulder and arm went on vacation, where they'd remained for months. Everything worked well, though. Thank you Lord.

On the way to Ft. Myers, I'd thought about my dad some; talked to my son-in-law on the phone; and visited my first cousin, the former Lynn Causey, and her teenage daughter Jade, in Sarasota. Lynn grew up in Amite County, and cut her swimming teeth in the spring-cold water of Walker Creek which runs under Highway 24 between Gloster and Liberty.

After our boat trip, Jerry and I had a great lunch at Appleby's. The 2 for $20 deal there was too good for cheap ole codgers like us to turn down, anyway.

During the day, three of my four kiddos dialed in. This morning, I'm busy at the lawyer's office disinheriting the fourth.

So what was my 10% in a day like yesterday? En route home during more than three hours, it poured rain in heavy traffic over a construction-filled stretch of Interstate 75. Twice. And one of those was for 15 miles.

There were cats and dogs all over my car. I drove by three accidents, and personally dialed 911 for one, since it happened right in front of me. At least the lady wasn't hurt.

It's amazing that some drivers slow down, but others simply turn on emergency flashers and continue driving 70 mph or more. The emergency they seem to be signaling is their driving.

Just kidding about the disinheritance. That son is deaf and phone calls are a bit more complicated, and I found his e-mail when I got home. Besides, the cost of the legal paperwork would probably be more than he'd get from my savings.

Yesterday's last blessing from our All-Mighty God was a safe trip in bad weather! I hope your Father's Day was as good or better, whether back home or out and about.


## IT'S ALL ABOUT FAMILY

My grandfather George Pollard Anders was one of several children, five or six according to memory, and when I'd ask where the family was from in Amite County, he'd gesture towards the west and say: "Out that way." From what he'd say, somewhere north of Gloster was a good guess. He said a brother had been a medical doctor but had died young. Of smallpox, I believed I'd been told.

These vague recollections were stuck within me, along with a desire to do some family research sometime down the road to find out more. The curiosity was there but the time hadn't been taken to find out.

Attending the Amite County Historical & Genealogical Society June 9th, Ms. Eva Frances Phares of Clinton, LA, told me she had a book of "Connections" already published that might help. I purchased that book and four others. Within an hour or so, later that night, I'd learned a lot in that very short time.

Out there, north of Gloster. Our family came from North Carolina, to Georgia, to Mississippi. In North Carolina, the spelling had probably been "Andrews". My great grandparents were identified, as were my great great grandparents, who were born in the early 1800s. "Out there, north of Gloster" turned out to be the Bewelcome community. Later the family moved to five miles northeast of Liberty, out along where Hwy 569 is now.

My grandfather Anders was one of 10 children, not five or six. As I read the names, I could recall his voice saying them and remember visiting with perhaps four of them across time. I'd always wondered about the one who was a doctor, had no clue where he was buried. At what age did he die? Of what? The

Connections book told me he'd passed away in 1906 of yellow fever, not smallpox. And he was buried then in...Gloster, in Roseland Cemetery. His name was John Rogers Anders, his wife was Mattie. He was just 26.

A few months ago on a Sunday morning, I'd casually strolled through Roseland and noticed a few last names like mine. One was very close to the Roseland Cemetery sign. So I returned, walked about 60 feet to the northeast, and there was great uncle John Rogers Anders and wife Mattie! She passed away in 1957. But he'd been there since 1906, 106 years, and I didn't have a clue, even though I'd looked at the tombstone earlier this year.

The Connections book told me more. He'd died of yellow fever, perhaps in South America, but likely in Panama. During the late 1800's, about the time he was born, the French began construction of the Panama Canal, but eventually gave up. In 1904, the United States took over, and completed the canal in 1914. Thousands of canal workers died of yellow fever. Many U. S. medical personnel went to help fight that disease. It's likely that great uncle John was one of them.

I doubt that my family history is more than a passing interest to you, and that's as it should be. What's important is your own. The point is...the Historical & Genealogical Society of Amite County is a great thing to participate in if you want to learn about your background. I guarantee you'll find the information interesting, even if you're not caught up in family research.

*Grave marker of John and Mattie Anders,
Roseland Cemetery, Gloster, Mississippi.*

For example, consider the following story. Actual names have been left out since descendants may still live here and there's no need to embarrass anyone.

"A lady of Amite County married a man of Amite County, in 1862. They divorced. She wasn't acting in accordance with his standards for a wife, so he took her out in a boat with intentions of letting her accidentally drown. After she promised to be a better more submissive wife, he guided the boat back to shore. As the boat neared shallow water, she jumped out of the boat and fled to safety."

Accidentally drown? Not too surprising they divorced, is it? If you don't find that story thought- provoking, you're living a more exciting life than I am. Things don't really change much across the years, do they?

## PRAYING IN EARNEST

One thing we learned while growing up in Amite County was how to pray. As life has progressed, I've discovered why that is important. On more than one occasion.

One time, I was alone, flying to San Antonio, Texas, from Baton Rouge. Over Orange, Texas, underneath me was a shipyard where WWII surplus Liberty ships were moored, being scrapped.

I leaned over from the pilot's seat and studied them with binoculars, through the passenger window. All that motion caused vertigo, one of a pilot's worse enemies. Uh oh, I thought, this is not good.

I put my head down for 30 seconds and let the airplane fly itself, meanwhile desperately praying: "God, I need your help here. If you want me, you've got me. I'm in your hands. Please." Lifting my head, the vertigo was still there. I put my head down again, and prayed the same prayer, but this time in CAPITAL LETTERS, with exclamation points!!!

Slowing sitting upright the second time, after a minute - my head was clear, the vertigo gone. Then, I just said three words: "Thank you, Lord." For whatever reason, God listened and granted my plea.

*1952 Cessna 170B, N2259D, my favorite airplane!*

Did you turn on the Discovery Channel on Sunday night, June 23rd, and see Nik Wallenda's successful walk over the tight rope across a gorge of the Grand Canyon?

The liberal media will downplay it - they already have - but Nike Wallenda put his training, courage and experience on the line and mixed in an extra ingredient that allowed him to do it safely. It was the all-mighty power of God and Jesus. What an example for the world it was! And the world was tuned in.

The wire was 1500 feet high and about that long, and Wallenda made the walk in just under 23 minutes, with winds gusting dangerously. He used no viewable safety net or tether. As he stepped out over the height of the canyon, he said something like, wow, what a view!

While walking, he was supposed to chat with Discovery Channel hosts and his father, his safety director. But he soon told his father he didn't want to talk to anyone. He even cautioned his dad to stop telling him how long he'd been on the wire. Instead, he immediately and fervently invoked his unseen safety net, his tether. Every step was timed with words like: "Jesus Jesus Jesus. Hallelujah! You are my savior. Please calm these winds, God. You have the power. You are everything to me, God. Please Jesus please. I trust you."

I don't have the words in exactly the right order but if you saw the walk, you know that Nik Wallenda literally prayed his way across that canyon. His strength and courage were perfectly held together by his plea for help to God, who was right there for him. Even just watching, it was an amazing experience. And Nik wasn't the only one praying.

Mr. Wallenda was wired for sound and the Discovery Channel couldn't mute his words. We all saw and heard a young man of faith and daring who believes in the power of our Heavenly Father. The most the hosts would say at the conclusion was to commend "his spirit". They just had to be politically correct, I suppose, but they experienced something they won't forget, either.

What an example Nik Wallenda was! Thank you, All-Mighty God, for letting us be able to talk to you directly, and for receiving and honoring Mr. Wallenda's prayer.

# Chapter 16

---

# Patiently Talkin' Chikin'

## FIELD MEMORIAL HOSPITAL

THE NEW FIELD Memorial Hospital being built in Centreville is great news for our area.

During my first two years at LSU, I worked 35 hours a week at Baton Rouge General Hospital. That time was spent in the business office. Two friends also were employed there. We checked patients out who were being discharged at night. We calculated insurance coverage and had the patient pay for what wasn't covered, or make arrangements to do so.

Then, some people carried additional policies and wanted extra copies of the bill. There was no "coordination of benefits" between companies, so folks often "double or triple" filed and made money on having been sick.

Computers weren't around. We had posting machines, and of course 10 key adding machines and regular typewriters. Those posting machines had a handle like a stick shift in a car. After you became proficient, you could really make them sing! In the early to middle 1960s, the hospital had 600 patient beds.

I remember the room rates well, because I posted thousands of them. A semi-private room was $16.50 a day; a private one, $21.00. Comprehend that in today's world!

The hospital administrator's name was Mr. Warren Huckaby. My sister, Faye, was his secretary for several years. I believe that's why it occurred to me to apply for employment in the first place.

It amazes me that people often think of a job as just a place to work and earn money. At BRGH, we had lots of fun! A hospital environment was a fine place to work. And I could always eat good food for a reasonable price in the cafeteria, quite a benefit for a hungry college student.

While at LSU, I needed hernia surgery, and the chief of staff at BRGH, a fun person whom I'd gotten to know, was my surgeon. Just before I got the knock-out juice, he told me he'd be assisted by Dr. Savage. I thought he was kidding. Until later, when I got a bill for $300. From Dr. Savage!

I was very busy with ROTC and additional courses as a junior and senior, so sought another job with fewer hours. I found work at a Holiday Inn on Airline Highway, close to where Earl K. Long Hospital is now. There I spent 24 hours a week. My boss was Mr. Dennis Hima, a retired Navy officer. He and his wife were really nice people. If you want to learn a lot about life, work in a place that rents beds. But that's a whole 'nother story!

After graduation, I had a year's wait until Air Force active duty began. The hospital needed an Assistant to sit in for the Personnel Director, Mr. Tom Terry, who was to conduct a half million dollar fund drive for hospital expansion. That was a lot of money then.

So I applied, was hired, and worked another year, and really got great experience. Then it was the military and life in general for several years. When I'd return to Baton Rouge, though, a stop at BRGH to visit friends was always in order. Mr. Terry was an AA member who had sorted out his life, and was one of the most influential mentors I ever had. Though he's long been gone to the land beyond the stars, I've never forgotten him.

Many citizens of this area have worked at Field Memorial Hospital, and many local folks have been treated there, who have the same kind of feelings about it. As a little boy, I remember visiting my Grandmother Carrie Rice, who was a patient at Field.

Good luck to those who build and staff the new facility in Centreville, and thank you for what you do!

## GREEN EGGS AND HAM

From the first grade at Liberty Elementary School, I remember just bits and pieces of a couple of books. One was about Jack and Jill going up a hill to fetch a pail of water. Someone fell down, I think, and broke their crown, and someone else came tumbling after. Another book was about Dick and Jane and their dog Spot, but I don't remember the plot.

Dr. Seuss books didn't really make their appearance in schools for a few more years, into the middle 1950s and beyond, but they made a splash when they did. Many people now alive ate some virtual green eggs and ham.

Dr. Seuss' birthday just went around March 2nd. He would be 110. Yesterday, during a discussion with a Gloster resident, I thought of Dr. Seuss and a few things he asked us to think about ourselves, when we look in the mirror and see "you". Here's just one of them.

"Today you are You, that is truer than true. There is no one alive who is Youer then You."

Specifically, the Gloster citizen and I were discussing political leadership in our town.

Last year in April, I took a 1,700 mile cross-country trip from New Mexico to the Atlantic Ocean, on U. S. Highway 82. That trip took me through many little Gloster-like towns in Texas, Arkansas, Mississippi, Alabama and Georgia. From one to the next, one could see major differences, even in spaces of only 10 miles.

I stopped and looked at little museums, visited Chambers of Commerce, ate in little cafes. Asking and looking around, the conclusion I reached as to why towns were different - whether they had a museum - a progressive atmosphere - a vision - a Historical Downtown or just an old set of buildings - was leadership. Did the local elected leaders lead, follow, or get out of the way?

Are you a local leader? Have you looked in the mirror lately? What do you think of yourself at 3 AM, are you happy with yourself? Are you doing the best job for your citizens? Here's another piece of advice from Dr. Seuss:

"You have brains in your head. You have feet in your shoes. You can steer yourself in any direction you choose. You're on your own. And you know what you know. You are the guy who'll decide where to go."

We're counting on you, Mr. and Mrs. Leader.

Dr. Seuss had some advice for me and my feelings, too, as we consider how to proceed:

"They say I'm old-fashioned, and live in the past, but sometimes I think progress progresses too fast!"


## ON BEING WELL GROUNDED

Sometimes I complained about the red clay and dust present in Amite County while growing up. I became convinced that

I wanted, to the extent possible, to live on paved roads later in life.

Of course, many Amite County roads that used to be dirt and gravel now have hard surfaces. One good thing about red clay and the dirt from which our dust flies, whether it's paved or not, though, is that it all feels solid.

You can give me a home where the buffalo roam, but don't give me a home where the ground I stand on shakes or feels like Jello.

The last major earthquake in Mississippi was in 1811. It was so severe, the Mississippi River ran backwards for a period. Reelfoot Lake in Tennessee, close to the Mississippi River, was created by a depression that formed during that quake when the hole filled up with river water.

In 1931, a quake measuring 4.7 on the Richter scale had its epicenter in Mississippi. That was our last such event. It was centered in Batesville, Mississippi. Go straight north from Gloster in our SW corner to the NW corner of the state and you'll drive right into Batesville.

I got to thinking about how solid Mississippi is while reading about the man in Tampa, Florida, who was swallowed up by a sinkhole while resting in his bedroom. Florida is sort of like a sponge, and has lots of sinkholes.

In Maitland, Florida, a sinkhole 325 feet across was discovered in the 1960s as Interstate 4 was built. The highway was diverted around the area, but in 2008 workers began a $9 million project to fill and stabilize the hole. Engineers say a road can be put over it now without any problems. I wonder if those engineers will be the first people to drive over that road?

In Winter Park, Florida, in 1981, a sinkhole swallowed several sports cars, parts of two businesses, the deep end of an Olympic-size swimming pool and a three-bedroom house. It stretched about 350 feet across and caused $2 million in damages.

And in 2002, a sinkhole about 150 feet across and 60 feet deep swallowed oak trees, sidewalks and park benches near an apartment complex in western Orange County, Florida.

A decision hasn't been made as to whether to fill in the most recent sinkhole that killed the Florida man in Seffner, a suburb of Tampa. His body cannot even be recovered. What a horrible thing.

You might want to rethink that trip to Disneyworld.

When they say we Mississippians are well grounded, is this part of what they mean? Thank God for blessings large and small including solid ground.


## THINK CHIKIN'

Remember those brightly colored chicks we got for Easter? Little bitty things we called bitties. Their coloring wore off as they became a regular part of the backyard chicken crowd.

Growing up in rural Mississippi, we certainly ate our share of those chickens from the back yard. Usually they were fried or baked. Good stuff!

Before refrigeration was common, having that chicken meant you had other things to deal with. Yes, my young lovelies, chickens weren't born in a frozen packaged state, in Walmart or some other store.

My great aunt Myrtis Robinson, who'd obviously learned how as a child, was often the person I saw dealing with a chicken who'd be a dinner guest, usually in about an hour. Now that was fresh.

My Aunt Myrt would grab that chicken by the neck, give it a few wrings in the air, and then drop the detached head on the ground, as the headless chicken ran around the yard a couple of laps. It was an awesome thing to see. I always wondered what the chicken head was thinking as it saw its body doing a 100 yard dash, in a circle. "Something's horribly wrong here," was my best guess.

If you've got a few miles on you and they're not all highway miles, you've had that feeling, haven't you, just short of having your head actually detached? Maybe your mother or father or your wife or husband or a boss or the legal system or a preacher had you by the neck, etc.?

*L to R, author's grandparents Susie and George Pollard Anders; parents George Davis and Lucille Anders; and great aunt Myrtis Robinson, 1960.*

The result at the table, though, in the case of the recently departed chicken, was nearly always good. Old chickens, I think, were baked or boiled rather than fried to make them tender, more palatable.

My wife and I once got a chicken at the store that was so tough that even when she baked it, it was nearly inedible. That chicken must have been a weightlifter or the yard Kung Fu champion. Throwing away food isn't in my play list, but we had to toss that one, and were careful in the process not to hit somebody with it.

A couple of my friends ate so much chicken as kids, they

wouldn't touch it as an adult, unless almost starving. "No more yardbird for me!" they'd exclaim. Both told horror stories of being invited for a meal where chicken unexpectedly appeared on the table.

Early on in my career, I had a chance to work in the corporate headquarters of Church's Chicken, a terrific opportunity. But I heard the "c" word so often during the interview, I figured I'd be crowing or clucking and sporting feathers before two weeks were done, so I declined.

In Mississippi, there were chores associated with chickens that were guaranteed to give you important lessons in humility. The one I remember most clearly was my mother saying: "You're cleaning out the chicken house today." That job was a mess! That's a little joke but also an understatement.

Well, I could go on and on and usually do, but even though it's breakfast time, I'm already getting hungry for lunch. Let's see…KFC opens at 10 AM, I think? Haven't been there for a while, and suddenly I have a hankering. Imagine that.

God, at Easter, we thank you for the risen Christ. And for our other blessings which include Noah having put a couple of chickens on the ark. I just wonder one thing. Who had to clean up their cage while they were on the boat? Doing that and being seasick at the same time does not sound like a good thing.

## THE PROBLEM WITH THAT IS…

On Sunday, April 28th, at high noon, I crossed the 'finish line' of the U. S. Highway 82 RV trip I took two weeks to complete, from the mountains of New Mexico to the Atlantic Ocean. It was a great experience, a first-hand look at small town America.

I deviated off Highway 82 only once, for a trip from Columbus up to Tupelo in our state. Elvis's boyhood home interested me. Folks, that young man was born dirt-poor, in abject poverty. In 1935, the Presleys had a two room house and no, one of them wasn't a bathroom. As a baby, Elvis slept in a dresser drawer. The house had cost the family $180 to build, and within three years of his birth, they'd lost it since they couldn't make the payment.

"It's just got to get better," Elvis said at 13, when they moved to Memphis. Within 11 years, he was back visiting Tupelo as a star. Dreams can come true if we work at them.

Many Southern towns are very similar, both in appearance and in how they developed and have sometimes undeveloped. Many small communities were built around the 'town square' concept, a result of European influence. In Texas, I went through two such small towns that had active, busy downtowns. In between was a beautifully designed place that was like a ghost town.

There must have been 60 buildings in the one in the middle. Fifty-eight of there were empty. All three towns were too close together to have been that much different in matters of economy, of business, of income sources. In the empty one, the only two active businesses I saw were an art gallery and a café, and the café wasn't open at 5:30 pm.

Gloster, Liberty, Crosby, Centreville and Woodville were on

my mind as I observed and talked to Chamber of Commerce leaders and others. Jay Nauta said recently in a column and I agree: It must be about "let's give that a try" instead of "the problem with that is…" It must be about "can do" instead of "can't do".

Some church buildings have closed across the country, and it's interesting what's been done with them. It's not always that the church has ceased to exist, often it's because the congregation has built a new place of worship, a bigger, better place. In Tifton, Georgia, an old church made of red brick and next door to the public library had been made into an art gallery and museum.

"If a church can't be a church, what better use of it than a museum?" I thought, since the celebration of much of our country's history has to do with the development of Christianity in the community. The Georgia museum had a quiet, peaceful presence. And artwork displayed was interesting…a depiction of Bible stories such as the prodigal son, set in 1950s surroundings. The prodigal, being welcomed home by his father in coveralls, was standing next to a '52 Chevy pickup.

I thought of the red brick church building in Gloster, just a block off Main Street, sitting empty; of how badly Gloster needs a museum to celebrate its rich history; of the old printing equipment at the Wilk-Amite Record, in business since 1892 that could become an important part of such an effort. I'm hoping it's possible someone might say: "Let's give that a try…" instead of: "The problem with that is…".

God, we need your help here.

# Chapter 17

MOSTLY ABOUT MOTHERS

## IT WAS A WEDGIE THAT CONFIRMED MY LOVE

TODAY, ANY CREATIVITY I may possess concerning writing about life is dulled by the reality of the end of it. Reg Duncan, a good man and a good friend, passed away recently. Thank goodness I wrote about Reg's life this past March. He deserved the tribute. I was unable to attend his funeral. My sincere sympathy to his family. I will miss him.

When Reg died, I was in Louisiana at my mother's bedside. She was in a coma from a massive stroke. She was 87, of Reg Duncan's era. Summoned to the hospital about midnight one night, I was fortunate to be holding her hand five hours later when she died. I witnessed many deaths during a long law enforcement career. Many violent, many natural. My mother's was the most peaceful, the most serene I have ever seen. I asked God to take her and I know He did.

Many have already experienced the loss of a parent; if you haven't, you will. Not a fun thing. But as my mother's last piece of life's puzzle fell into place, I reflected on her time on this good earth. A very good time. She was a Mississippi country girl, one of nine siblings. Only a brother and sister are left. Her maiden name was Rice. Her daddy - my grandfather - said they were of the long grain variety, the best kind, he said. She knew the value and rewards of hard work. She picked corn and cotton, hoed the garden as a youngster.

She was my own father's right hand, the record keeper, paymaster, income tax preparer as he owned sawmills, machine shops, the ice plant. She was the glue that held our family together. If life was to be described as a baseball game, she was home base. She was generous, she was funny. She wasn't sweet, she could be outspoken. Even the preacher said that at her funeral. She was always our disciplinarian. The only possible good thing I could imagine about her hands being stilled at last was that they couldn't go back and whack my butt again.

I always loved her but an incident that happened when I was about 10 confirmed my love for her forever.

A self-appointed church policewoman, a very large lady, sat near us young kids on the back row at Liberty Baptist to keep us quiet. (I still sit on the back row; they won't let me sit in the parking lot.) She stood up in front of us, sporting an amazing wedgie. Don't know what a wedgie is? Good grief. Ask a teenager in your family, they'll tell you. Misbehaving in church was a capital felony in our family. But we saw an astounding sight, too funny to resist breaking out in hysterics. The preacher stopped the sermon, called us down, made us go sit with our parents.

On the way home, my mother said through gritted teeth: "NOW - JUST - WHAT - WAS - SO - FUNNY?" I think there was a non-church word between so and funny. With thoughts of English dungeons, the rack, the hedge bush switch I was about to meet up close and personal...I described what we saw that caused the commotion. My mother knew the lady in question, got a vision. A tiny smile slowly formed at the corners of her mouth. Then we all laughed, uncontrollably, and have to this day about it. When she smiled, I knew I'd survive the incident, and I saw her fairness, her understanding, her humor shine through. I've loved her unquestionably ever since.

Aside from religious values, her teaching to us was: "Do what's right and you'll be all right." No matter what, I've tried to live by that motto and know what? She was right. I've been all right.

My thanks to my wonderful stepfather, Don, for his 18 years of love and devotion to her. No one could have done more. My appreciation to a young nurse, DeLyn, who was there with us. I'm not sure how she and her colleagues do what they do but I appreciate it.

My mother was a seamstress for many years, a professional who worked in ladies' department stores. She made clothing from scratch for at least two Louisiana governors' wives, for comedienne Phyllis Diller among others. Her skills were sought after.

Her hands were twisted and bent from such work, and from arthritis. But as I held them, even as she died, they were still soft and warm. At the end, I imagined I could hear the sound of an old Singer sewing machine starting up in heaven.

Thank you, Mother. Rest in peace.

*Author with his mother, Lucille Rice Anders, 1950,*
*photo taken at the Bungalow Inn in Liberty, Mississippi.*

## HEY MA! THINKING OF YOU...
## HOPE YOU'RE STILL DANCIN'!

> "There's a church in the valley in the wildwood
> No lovelier place in the dell
> No spot is so dear to my childhood
> As the little brown church in the dell"

Many of you recognize the words from the old song, Church in the Wildwood. James Canyon Church near Cloudcroft, New Mexico, with its small, quiet cemetery, is such a place. As a community, we've visited there often lately. Too often, it seems.

Sometime before May 9th, I'll visit a similar spot - be it a little flatter - in rural Mississippi. It'll be a Mother's Day visit. This will be my second such occasion without my mother, and I miss her.

The little country church where she's buried is dear to my childhood. My great-grandparents donated the land, and as a youngster I was a frequent visitor. At her grave site, I'll focus on the good times we had.

My mother was adventuresome and fun, a bit zany. Here's one escapade I'll always remember. Inadvertently, it determined a significant portion of my future, and my children's futures as well.

She took my sister and me on our first airplane ride. Oh...it was her first plane ride, too. My dad worked in Central America - Honduras - in the 1950s. We planned to spend the summer of 1953 with my father in the small village of Guaimaca. He had a lumber camp there, about 80 kilometers northeast of Honduras' capital, Tegucigalpa.

We obtained passports in New Orleans, returned later to travel to Honduras on TACA Airlines, still in operation today. Laying on a motel room bed the night before our flight, we studied Spanish. I was a nervous and excited 10 year old who didn't sleep too well.

My dad wanted my mother to bring his German Luger pistol. "How can I get it through customs?" she asked. "With a couple of cartons of Camels," he replied, "no problem." Mordida - the bribe, the little bite - was an established practice. She carried the gun in a big purse, underneath the cigarettes.

I recall the aircraft being a Lockheed Constellation, a curvy sleek-looking four engine propeller-driven craft. (I had no clue that 13 years later I'd be flying across Vietnam to Taiwan on the same type of Air Force plane when an engine would fail. The Connie, though, was sometimes called the World's Finest Trimotor and returned us safely to Thailand. I still didn't like the sight of that stationary prop out the window, or the thought of guys named Charlie looking up, salivating.)

Back in 1953, our first stop was in Belize. No problem there. Next was Guatemala City, Guatemala. Just our luck...we landed in the middle of an attempt to overthrow the government. Herded into a room at the airport, we were held for a couple of hours, couldn't leave. "Oh, well," I thought, "Mother has the Luger." Yeah, watch yourself, rebels, don't mess with my ma.

The room had large windows that overlooked the runway. Guatemalan Air Force P-51 Mustangs - most likely U. S. WWII surplus fighter aircraft - were taking off with bombs attached, returning without them. Someone on the ground was having a whole lot more fun than we were. I was in the middle of a revolution, yet had complete confidence in my mother to keep me safe. Aren't mothers something?!

Finally allowed to leave, we arrived at our destination, Tegucigalpa. Only later in life did I learn it's one of the world's most dangerous airports. Surrounded by mountains, with a short runway, it requires very steep landings and takeoffs. But - what, me worry? - hey, my mom was there. With her Luger. And the cigarettes. We cleared customs as the inspector lit up the Camels.

What a fantastic summer! I hung out with native boys at the sawmill camp. Played with Richard, our parrot, and Chico, our monkey. (Monkeys are cute, aren't they?...but are very mischievous. Some things they do shouldn't be allowed. Like R-rated movies, no child under the age of 17 should be allowed to have one, unless his parents are present. The term "wild monkey" is still with me.)

We slept in hammocks. Visited banana plantations in our jeep, kept a stalk of fresh bananas hanging in the camp house. My mother used Pet condensed milk in cereal in place of fresh milk; made flapjacks that we ate with Karo syrup, the only kind available. We went to an occasional movie - with English sub-titles – in Tegucigalpa. Back then, the capital city had three neon signs.

Returning to the U. S., the flight was mostly routine. Guatemala was quiet. Over New Orleans, though, we encountered thunderstorms, circled the airport for more than an hour before finally landing safely. Hey, I was then the experienced air traveler, thanks to my mother's reassuring presence!

You know...it's just now occurred to me that my mother - on her first plane ride too – with adult realization of the danger of being caught up in political turmoil, war - sneaking a gun through customs – flying near thunderstorms - was probably very frightened too...but maintained a calm demeanor for the sake of my sister and me.

That trip ignited my curiosity and interest in aircraft that persists to this day in our family. I became a commercial pilot, flew police helicopters. My sons were introduced to aviation in a small Cessna we had. My eldest became a Navy fighter pilot, is now an airline pilot. My middle son, born deaf, enjoyed parachuting. The youngest served as an Army helicopter Aero Scout.

At age seven, my daughter rode in her first helicopter. She carries my mother's first name as her middle name, incidentally. Iris. A beautiful flower.

My mother took her final flight on July 11, 2008, on the wings of angels. I was blessed to be holding her hand at the gate, as she boarded. If the Good Lord will let me repeat that routing someday, my mother will be at the other end, waiting. I just hope they made her check her Luger at the Pearly Gate, or she'll be shooting in the air.

Cowboys want to be buried with their boots on, right? Well, my mother wasn't a cowgirl, but she wanted to be buried with her red high-heeled shoes - her dancin' shoes - so she could "dance in heaven". Her early religious training frowned on dancing, but my mother was...well...my mother.

Just before her casket was sealed, I put those red shoes inside. My stepfather told me tearfully later that day...when they'd watch the Lawrence Welk show, my mother would say: "Close the blinds, Don. Dance with me." He died six weeks later, partly of illness, mostly of a broken heart. I hope they're still dancin'.

If your mom is still around, will you give her an extra hug on Mother's Day? For those of us who've lost ours. We'll appreciate that, and I bet we'll feel a nice little squeeze the exact moment you do. Thanks, and Happy Mother's Day!


## MOTHERHOOD

This is a Mother's Day after action report. How did your day go? I hope your mother is alive and well so that you enjoyed her company. Mine left this earth in 2008 for a better place. I thought about her and felt her presence. She'd be 93 if still alive.

Our Sunday School class read scripture that celebrated motherhood. Then each of us told favorite stories about our mothers. Some were funny, some were about how they took care of us and taught us. It was a great class. People were reluctant at first but we got into it, and the time went by too fast.

We can't live fulltime in Amite County because we need to be near my wife's mother, who will be 90 in July. Her best friend, Marie, is 91. Each lost their husband a few years back. Each has a "man friend" with whom they attend dinners, plays, and such. Neither has any plan to remarry.

My wife had a shrimp boil for Kathryn - her mother, and Marie. It's an annual get-together at our home. Marie has a son in North Carolina but no relatives near where she lives so we always invite her. Marie's upbringing taught her to bring a small gift for such occasions, although we assure her it isn't necessary. She brought a kalanchoe plant, which has beautiful yellow flowers. It's already planted in my wife's flower garden.

Something led us into a discussion of war. Two of Kathryn's four children are retired military. Her son, Jay, was a B-52 pilot. Her daughter was a career Army officer. Both had their adventures but came through intact.

Marie had twin sons, Eugene and Edward. Eugene enlisted or was drafted into the Army and served in Vietnam under tough conditions. Per Marie: "He went over as an innocent 17 year old boy and came back as a very ill man who could have been 40. He'd lost all his hair. He was rescued from a field of battle very seriously wounded, with large ants crawling over him."

Marie explained that her son, back home, would turn the water on in the kitchen sink and simply stare at it running for long periods of time, and would become angry if his father turned it off. Eugene died of Agent Orange complications years ago, but Marie hasn't forgotten him, and she maintains a degree of unhappiness with LBJ over his conduct of the war in Vietnam.

But all of that was a small part of a great day, and a mother has the right to remember her children on Mother's Day. After all, without them, there'd be no such event. We watched the movie "Mama Mia", a fun musical, which "the girls" enjoyed. It was great to have them over, and my wife and I will be reminded of the event when we look at the very pretty yellow flowers of the kalanchoe plant.

Thank God for motherhood and all it means to all of us.

## LAST CROSS COUNTRY RIDE
## OF THE MICHIGAN SAILOR BOY

I love living. I love life. Been lucky enough to have canoed the Lower Canyons of the Rio Grande, bathed in the remote hot springs there. Eaten hotcakes and bacon at a chuck wagon breakfast at the Pendleton Roundup in Oregon in cold weather, savored the hot coffee.

Paddled across a bay on the Texas coast at midnight, the water so calm that when I looked up at the Milky Way, it made me dizzy. Later, held onto the boat in the same stretch of water for hours, in tornado-type winds and waves, wondering if Les and I would make it, then cherished the experience. Picked up my father in my own small airplane, flown across two states without a map, yet confident of where we were going and where we'd end up. Marveled at the majesties of the Grand Canyon, the Meteor Crater.

These are just a tiny fraction of life's blessings I've savored, tasted, enjoyed. To me the glass is really half full. Life is about living, adventuring, celebrating. It's just too short, goes by too fast.

Somewhat reluctantly, then, I write about someone's death for the fourth time this year, risking that you may think I'm focused on sad things. The last was about my mother, Lucille Green, back in July. I had to do that. She gave me life, teaching and a sense of humor to blend it successfully. But now my wonderful stepfather, Donald Green, has died. On August 30th, just 50 days after my mother left. They were married either 14 or 18 years. Someday I'll explain that. I think they had a little secret.

Previously, I've mentioned Don and his WWII adventures as a US Navy sailor. He was on a cruiser, the USS Memphis, served in the Atlantic Theatre, was an engineman. Like many patriotic young people of his day, he enlisted just after Pearl Harbor. Off the coast of Africa, he was the crane operator selected to hoist President Roosevelt aboard, FDR in his wheelchair. FDR, who told Don to his face: "Son, that was the best elevator ride I've ever had!"

He was the only machinist who volunteered to try to make a critical part for a British ship that couldn't keep up in a convoy, dead meat for a submarine attack. A British ship whose captain sent personal thanks to Don on behalf of his crew. The part had worked. How many children, grandchildren, great grand-children of English sailors may not have tasted life but for his efforts?

He was a retired Michigan firefighter, a retired Fire Chief. At work he was "Dozer". Did you have a job that needed doing? A door that needed breaking down during the height of a fire? A ladder that had to be climbed? Dozer would do it. Dozer did it. Dozer couldn't be stopped. He was your man. He worked at, retired from, the same fire station in Ypsilanti, Michigan, as his father.

He was creative, he was a perfectionist. He was Michigan's state fire inspector. He founded his own business, Hobby Printing, which turned into much more than a hobby. His sons learned the printing trade. Two are still in it after 30 plus years.

Did this sailor ever make calls to the beautiful New Mexico area we lived in? Recalled to the Navy during the Korean War, he helped fire 10 rockets from White Sands Missile Range, lived in Las Cruces. Three of his children were born in El Paso. Years later, he and my mother visited Cloudcroft, stayed at the Spruce Cabins.

As for all of us, his oceans weren't always smooth. After a di-vorce, he moved to Florida, later to Louisiana where a son lived. A son who lived close to where my mother lived. Don, a divorced man, became a deacon in the church my mother at-tended. He gave two women a ride to church. My mother - one of them - sat in the back seat. One day he picked her up first, told her: "Get in the front seat today." "Won't so-and-so be mad?" my mother asked. "Doesn't matter", said Don.

My mother never left his front seat until July 11th, this year.

Almost 87, he had many medical problems, but will power and determination kept him alive to take care of my mother. He truly loved her. I drove him on his last cross-country trip, up through the heartland of America, to live with his family, to reunite. He cried when we crossed the Michigan state line. "I'm home", he said. He was kind of nervous about it. "Better days are ahead, Mr. Don", I told him. His doctor in Louisiana always called him Mr. Don. I had kind of picked up the habit.

He did okay for about a week, then went downhill rapidly. At the hospital, a respirator was used to keep him going. After a couple of times, off and on, he said: "Leave it off. I just want to be with Lucille." They did. He is.

At his funeral, one son played taps, another preached. Beautifully. It was for "Dad", not some stranger. He was buried in his Navy uniform, the one he had worn proudly, bravely. He was my dad, my sister's dad, too, for 18 years. My daughter's grandfather, the only one she ever really knew. So long, Mr. Don. Thank you, Sailor Boy. Thanks to your family for sharing.

With all my heart, I believe God told him: "Good work, Donald Green. Better days are here, enjoy! Love you, boy."

# Chapter 18

━━━∞━━━

# FLY ME AWAY

## WHEN DREAMS ARE REALIZED

**ALL YOUNG BOYS** growing up in Mississippi – girls too – had their dreams. We saw farming and cattle and trees and sawmilling but some of us developed other ideas about our futures. Seeing airplanes overhead and getting involved with them caused me to seriously wonder if I could ever fly one. Even perhaps to make a living?

A visit to the Crosby Airport at age seven, a flight to Honduras and back at age 10, and moving to Oregon where I met a classmate whose father had owned an airplane in Alaska motivated me. My Oregon friend, at 12, had learned to fly his dad's plane. If he could do it, why couldn't I? My bicycle and I became frequent visitors to the Ashland, Oregon, airport. I hoped to get a ride but not all wishes, of course, come true.

Later, the military was in need of pilots for Vietnam and while getting shot at wasn't too welcoming, the opportunity to fly overcame that concern so I applied for Air Force pilot training. A minor eyesight issue stopped me. But later in the military I received my private pilot's license, then attended a commercial flight school and earned certificates to operate both airplanes and helicopters.

All that led to a commercial flying job in East Texas, and later to a job as a police helicopter pilot in San Antonio, Texas. The five years I flew choppers were the happiest working days of my life, the most fun job I ever had. I couldn't believe I got paid to do it.

*Mississippi country boy living his childhood dream, 1980.*

My four children knew many of the things I did since they were there. But my 12 grandchildren only know me as Grandpa, the ole timer who's nice to them and sends birthday cards. I wanted to leave a record of my earlier life for them and friends, so my project this past winter was to write a book called "FOXTROT, WE'RE ON THE WAY! ...San Antonio, Texas, Police Department Helicopter Stories, a Memoir..." It was published this past May 20th.

Here's some back cover information:

"Dashing to a police helicopter, quickly firing it up, and responding to an emergency call with, 'Foxtrot, we're on the way!' was a dream realized...

True stories - real life drama! - of Foxtrot, the San Antonio, Texas, Police Department aviation unit formed in the 1970s, today called Blue Eagle... Between 1975 and 1981, the author, a police officer and commercial pilot, helped pioneer the use of helicopters in law enforcement. There were few universal procedures. Flight crews raced to intercept high speed chases, searched for homicide victims, and engaged in a few shenanigans. Read these actual accounts and more... The Day I Bombed Salado Creek - The Body That Didn't Get Away - The Night the Lights Went Out - Sex and the Single Helicopter Pilot - The Dream That Went Bad - The Angry Go-Away Arm - The Shot Not Heard 'Round the World! Learn about early leaders in Sgt. Jarke's Final Chapter, and Cedar Posts & Sardines. Dangers are spotlighted in Today Isn't a Good Weather Day, and What Was That Noise? Sum it all up with Burglar on the Roof, Joy in the Heart!"

The book is available on-line at Amazon.com, Barnes&Noble.com, and at OutskirtsPress.com/bookstore. And yes, it's a for-profit book, but all profits will go to Crossing Borders Ministries of Fabens, Texas, missionary friends along the Texas/Mexico border.

God has been very good to my old flying unit. For more than 40 years, there has never been a serious injury. It seems only fair to pay Him back. I hope you'll buy and read the book and help my friends. I hope to have book signings in Gloster and Liberty soon and I'll have copies with me.

## LEADERS WANTED

I was born in Amite County, moved away at the age of 12, and stayed gone for more than 50 years. Among other things, I had a police career of more than 30 years and a military career of 28 years, most of that as a reservist.

During those careers, I had the following experiences, up close and personal. In the Air Force, Master Sergeant Glen Lee took me under his wing, showed me the ropes. When my wife was seriously ill, Lt Colonel Clarence Dixon took time from a busy schedule to visit us when others didn't.

During my police service, a man attacked me with a machete. My vice detective partner, Jerry Pittman, who was born near Jackson, may have saved my life when he stopped the attacker. On another occasion, a hostage taker took an infant captive and held a shotgun to the baby's head. Just Detective Anthony Linson and I were there. Anthony, who was closer, laid down his weapon and confronted the man, who finally handed him the baby.

It was the bravest act I ever witnessed a police officer do, who lived through it. The hostage taker killed himself a few minutes later with the same weapon. In another incident, Sergeant Willie Walker took a .357 magnum bullet in the head but lived, and later courageously stood up for me during a situation where I needed help.

Lee, Dixon, Pittman, Linson and Walker are all black men. If I didn't know it already, I learned that you don't judge a book by its cover. The color of a man or woman's skin doesn't determine quality, integrity, courage or the ability to lead. And God determines the circumstances of our birth, we don't.

Having said that, I ask you to vote for Alderman Bill Adams for Mayor of Gloster next week. Why? I'm not a fulltime resident or voter. But I do have a substantial financial investment in Gloster since I financed the sale of the paper to Casey Campbell and retained ownership of the building, thus I pay taxes here. My money is where my mouth is.

The current mayor simply has not been responsive to our requests for information, comments or material requested for your benefit as readers. He stopped submitting a mayor's column more than a year and a half ago. Mayor Stratton of Liberty is responsive. Mayor Lee of Centreville is responsive, but Gloster's mayor is not.

The poor handling of the Chief of Police situation cost you, the taxpayer, an unnecessary wad of money, and that's just one example.

Alderman Adams always showed up on short notice for such news events as the opening of a new business when the Mayor did not.

Black voters, of course, outnumber others by two to one. It's this simple: Unless many persons vote along lines other than racial, Alderman Adams will not be elected.

During a recent cross-country trip across hundreds of small Southern towns in Texas, Arkansas, Mississippi, Alabama and Georgia, many of which have a majority black population, I paid close attention to those that are doing well and those that aren't. The successful ones had good leadership, regardless of the color of the leader.

Nationally, I've been disappointed that Colin Powell or Condoleezza Rice haven't thrown their hats into the ring. I'd support either in a heartbeat.

For Gloster's sake, on June 4th, choose like your future depends on it, since it probably does. These are tough times, requiring open and effective leadership. May God bless America, and all the people of Gloster, Mississippi.


## STONE MOUNTAIN, GEORGIA

On October 23rd, my wife and I will pull our small travel trailer to Stone Mountain, Georgia, for a Country Living Fair. This is a repeat of a trip from two years ago, and we'll meet friends from North Carolina that we made on the previous outing.

My wife will be mostly touring the Country Living displays and I'll mainly be looking at Civil War sites in the area. Country Living's event is great, but to me it's mostly a giant garage sale and I've got enough "stuff". In my wife's defense, she just likes to look, and gets lots of decorating ideas.

Stone Mountain, close to Atlanta, is a quartz monzonite dome monadnock - no kidding - and its elevation is almost 1,700 feet. It stands out in the flat area like a giant toadstool. We'll probably hike to the top again, and ride the Skyride. On the latter, one gets a fantastic view of a carving in the east side of the mountain of Stonewall Jackson, Robert E. Lee, and Jefferson Davis.

Confederate Hall is a museum in the park that shows a historical documentary about the Civil War called "The Battle for Georgia". I like to visit places where significant Civil War events took place. If time permits, I want to see the Atlanta Cyclorama and Civil War Museum. The Cyclorama, a 365-degree mural painted in 1885 - 1886, depicts the Battle of Atlanta.

The Cyclorama gets great reviews, but I wonder if I'll brave Atlanta traffic to go there. Atlanta and Houston, Texas, traffic are first - that means worst - in my book of places I travel through somewhat frequently, and I try to avoid such mayhem. We shall see. Los Angeles, California, also known for such congestion, is off my usual route.

On the Internet, there are dating sites for farmers, seniors, Christians, those who are harmonious, etc. Sometimes I think I'll establish one for people in traffic, and let drivers trade families/dogs/jobs/houses and the like with those who are feverishly going the other direction. Then nearly everyone can stay home since there won't be the need to dash around like people do.

That unlikely dream aside, here's hoping a future excursion will allow us to visit Franklin, Tennessee, where the Battle of Franklin took place. It's my understanding that many Amite Countians lost their lives there during the Civil War. The Amite County Historical and Genealogical Society will have a historical program on that battle at their meeting in Liberty on Saturday, November 8th, at 10 am. I urge you to attend!

My wife and I are grateful to God for the blessings that allow us to make such journeys.


## ABRAHAM LINCOLN'S PERSONAL RULES OF CONDUCT

Visiting Stone Mountain, Georgia, last week, I drove into Atlanta to look at the Cyclorama, a circular mural depicting one day in the Battle of Atlanta during the Civil War.

The day represented is July 22, 1864. The painting was made by 11 German artists. It took 22 months to complete. There are just 16 cycloramas in the world, four of them in the United States.

The mural is almost 400 feet long if spread out, 42 feet high (the world's tallest oil painting), and is done on Belgian linen. It's well taken care of with periodic cleaning and touch-ups. It originally cost about $1100 and is now valued at $25 million. Wish I had a half dozen of them. I'd sell five and keep just one. Then take you to lunch.

Thousands of soldiers on both sides are pictured. They're shown in scenes of war, alive or injured or dead. Only one woman is visible. She's a Confederate nurse. One black person is present. He's a former slave, sitting on a horse, watching the fighting. There's a single bird flying in the sky, an eagle that was the mascot of a Federal unit. It was turned loose and flew over every battle that regiment fought in.

Clark Gable and others of the film crew of "Gone with the Wind" visited the Cyclorama in 1936. Mr. Gable said it was a good work of art but would be better if he were in it. He was painted in as an injured Federal soldier, laying on his back. It's extremely unlikely you'd notice him unless he was pointed out, as our guide did.

The largest figure shown charging into battle on his horse is Federal General John A. Logan. Why? He originally commissioned the painting, intending to use it to help achieve his political ambition of becoming vice-president or even president. Politicians don't change much, do they? Unfortunately for General Logan, he caught pneumonia and died three years after the work was done but before it could aid him.

In the gift shop, I saw a poster for sale which lists Abraham

Lincoln's personal Rules of Conduct. I did a bit of research and found that Honest Abe was voted in a recent survey of 3,000 respondents as The Best President ever. Interestingly, George W. Bush, who catches all sorts of flack, finished fourth. Barrack Obama came in 18th. Go figure.

Since Mr. Lincoln is held up by so many as the Best President, and I don't necessarily disagree, it seems as if many more would follow his rules today. What are they?

1. The way for a young man to rise is to improve himself every way he can, never suspecting that anybody wishes to hinder him.

2. Let none falter who thinks he is right.

3. Quarrel not at all. No man resolved to make the most of himself can spare time for personal contention.

4. By all means, don't say "if I can", say "I will".

5. The fact is, truth is your truest friend no matter what the circumstances are.

6. Stand with anybody that stands right. Stand with him while he is right and part with him when he goes wrong.

7. Leave nothing for tomorrow which can be done today.

8. Better to remain silent and be thought a fool than to speak out and remove all doubt. (This is my personal favorite.)

9. I say "try". If we never try, we shall never succeed.

I've gone to Washington, D. C., several times, but have never seen this poster displayed.


**SEEING RED**

Like many veterans, you should have seen it in color.

"In Color" is a country song released in 2007. The artist is Jamey Johnson. I heard it today - Veteran's Day - on a country station as they honored veterans with patriotic music. It's the story of a grandfather describing old black and white photographs to his grandson, depicting the grandfather's experiences in World War II.

> "*This one here was taken overseas*
> *In the middle of hell in 1943, it was winter time*
> *You can almost see my breath*
> *That was my tailgunner, Ol' Johnny McGee*
> *A high school teacher from New Orleans*
> *And he had my back, right through the day we left*"

Yes, I'm a veteran, having served 28 years in the Air Force., most of them, though, as a reservist. When the Vietnam War was going hot and heavy, I volunteered for Southeast Asia, thinking it was my duty. But with the luck of the draw, I was assigned to Thailand, a country I hadn't really thought of as being involved.

In fact, it takes 10 support people for every front line combat soldier and I simply served a year in a support capacity, and never thought of myself as being in danger. Pilots flying from my base were certainly in harm's way, and many of them didn't come home. I saw the war in black and white, not in color like they did.

WWII, Korea, Vietnam, Iraq and Afghanistan, more. We've had plenty of wars, and they show no signs of letting up. Since WWII, politicians seem to figure out ways to start them, while not actually participating in them. They sit back while young men - and now women - go off to fight. Sometimes, of course, the reasons for war appear valid, and WWII was one of those times.

I didn't question Vietnam, it seemed only that if my friends were going, I should go too. Perhaps now I'm a little wiser about wars. My focus, though, on Veteran's Day isn't that, but being thankful for the life I've lived as a result of those who gave their all for us. I think of what I've had that they didn't.

I remember Pete Moak, a good Baton Rouge and LSU buddy killed in Vietnam. Of Grant Stewart, another friend from Baker, who died there. Pete was leading his Army platoon. Grant was flying his F-105 fighter-bomber over Laos. Oh, we didn't fight in Laos, did we? Tell Grant's family that.

It's ironic that I saw some things in color in the police service, right here in the United States, and not during a military career. My partner and I were ambushed and he was killed. The same assailant, who sent a .357 slug sailing up alongside my left

215

arm from wrist to elbow, almost spared you the reading of this story. It's impossible to explain things that happen in color to those who've only seen life in black and white. One has to just press on and be grateful for the goodness of the Good Lord and good training and good luck.

I offer my personal thanks to veterans to whom country singer Jamey Johnson was talking about when he ends his song with the last line of the chorus: "You should have seen it in color." The one that most often comes to mind is red. My appreciation goes to those who made it back, and to the families of those who didn't.

May God bless and preserve the United States of America!

# Chapter 19

$\infty$

# REMEMBERING UNCLE BERT, AND OTHER TALES

## SEE YOU LATER, ALLIGATOR

Growing up in Amite County, I saw wildlife in its environment, the wild. No animal I ever watched was having a free lunch. Few were involved in leisure. It was nearly always about survival. Usually it was about food gathering, and that included trying not to be eaten by the next biggest, meanest thing up the food chain.

This past week, my wife and I spent a few days at Wekiwa Springs State Park in Florida, just north of Orlando. The park is a 7,000 acre slice of old Florida, smack dab in the middle of a very urban area. Modern suburbs exist alongside the boundaries. But inside, you feel as if you're back in the 1800s. We hiked eight miles.

We saw one raccoon, one snake, two deer, a lot of squirrels, many turtles, numerous frogs, a variety of birds, and seven alligators. Like critters in Mississippi, all were involved in eating or finding something to eat. That was their primary activity. At some time, they all would be involved in some sort of breeding to further their species. Again, all about survival.

What we saw went on 24/7 and again, there was no free lunch. No Social Security, no Obamacare, no retirement plans. The "7", of course, includes Saturday and Sunday. Man seems to be the only living creature that expects to have free time to just enjoy himself. And more and more men expect to do so without having earned it, seemingly.

Come to think of it, I didn't see one creature texting or e-mailing or tweeting any other one. But I did see a lot of humans doing so. One lady going down the Wekiwa River in a canoe looked down the whole time, paying attention to her phone. Nature at its finest. Maybe she had an Animal Planet app on her I-Phone.

Some of the alligators we saw were taking nap time, or so it appeared. I'd guess, though, they were being still while digesting something. I saw some humans swimming within a few hundred feet of where my wife and I saw an eight foot gator. I asked my two little traveling companions, a fly and a flea that live in my shirt pocket, if they'd like to go for a swim.

Both were aghast. "Not I," said the fly. "Not me," said the flea. My wife and I declined, too. Alligators have a favorite swimming maneuver that we don't find particularly attractive. It's called the "death roll".

Using a canoe, we approached a couple of them carefully to just say hello.

05.21.2016 08:27

*"Come on in, the water's fine," says this Florida gator, 2016.*

Local residents who know the river told us there was a 12 foot male gator that was the daddy of all alligators in the area, his mate and the mother being a nine foot female. Daddy Gator supposedly is very territorial and prevents any intrusion onto his turf. All the smaller gators are supposedly their offspring.

My wife wondered where the young alligators found mates, if

all the local gators were brothers and sisters. "Maybe some are born with a wicked grin and buck teeth," she said, and we had a good laugh as we considered that, since all alligators have a wicked grin and buck teeth. Maybe it's because of marriage to a sister or brother. "Maybe that's why alligators don't kiss," I volunteered, "it's like kissing your sister."

Yes, the week in Florida before Thanksgiving was a slow one. Hope your Thanksgiving Day finds you eating a hard-earned and well deserved turkey dinner and not just a free lunch.

## WALTER THE DUCK

Are you a Duck Dynasty fan? The Robertsons of West Monroe, Louisiana, the stars of that show, have proved what we already knew…one can be a redneck and have fun and still make it big.

My wife grew up in New Jersey and surprisingly is a big fan. I think she has a crush on Uncle Si. She loves that it's "clean" fun and that the family prays at the end of the show. Recently, I noticed a new glass in our kitchen. "Fear the Beard", it says, on the side. She's been drinking a lot of iced tea from it.

Wouldn't Amite County's Jerry Clower have loved this program? Common sense and nonsense and God and country all mixed up together. The people in Duck Dynasty are the same kind of folks Jerry Clower told stories about.

In the opening of the program, I see that mallard duck

walking across in front of the family. It reminds me of Walter, the one duck I ever owned. Briefly.

A friend named Walter, got a duckling for his daughter for Easter. Remember those brightly colored baby chicks we used to get? How the color would grow out as they grew up, and you were left with just an ordinary chicken? This duckling started as a bright red.

Well, Walter's daughter's duck grew up in their backyard with just a tiny plastic toy pool to swim in. The duck kept growing, while the small pool stayed the same size. Fully grown and shed of its red color, the duck was a mallard with a bright green head. Eventually it could only take a paddle stroke or two in the little pool.

Walter knew that I lived at a lake. There were five other houses. The lake was about a half mile long by a quarter mile wide, and there were lots of ducks. But they were white ducks, and white and grey ducks, what I'd call ordinary ducks. There wasn't a green-headed duck amongst them. Walter asked if I'd take his duck and turn him loose there.

"Of course," I said. Maybe having a green-headed duck in the herd would provide a little variety. Walter and I worked together, so he brought his duck in one day and I took him home, my duck then. My kids promptly named the duck Walter after his former owner. Well, you've heard the saying: "Takes to it like a duck to water." While that's true, it's not always an instant thing.

Walter - the duck - promptly jumped into the lake. Immediately, minnows - seeing a new set of duck legs - started nibbling at his feet and he just as promptly jumped out. It took serious persuading to convince that mallard to enter the water again.

Eventually, though, Walter figured out the minnows were just messing with him and stayed in the water. The plain lady ducks really liked that gorgeous green head and within a few months, there were lots of mallards around the lake. Walter would occasionally swim by the house with his entourage and everything seemed - well - pretty ducky.

But a person who lived in one of the other five houses, a house across the lake, got tired of all the ducks about every three years and conducted a duck roundup. I guess he sold them. Walter got caught up in the next crackdown and went away to Duck Heaven. But it had been good to have Walter the mallard around for a few years and he left quite a legacy.

Watching Duck Dynasty, I remember Walter fondly.


## REST IN PEACE, UNCLE BERT

The obituary of Mr. James Bertrell Rice appeared in last week's paper. His funeral service was held on Monday, May 21st, at Plank Road Baptist Church just south of Clinton, Louisiana.

Mr. Bert, as many called him, was a week shy of being 89 years old. He was associated with his church for more than 50 years, serving as a deacon and Sunday School teacher and in other positions of responsibility.

He was one of nine children, a Liberty native. My mother was one of those nine children, so he wasn't Mr. Bert to me. He was Uncle Bert.

When he was about 14, he was diagnosed with Osteomyelitis, an infection of the bone or bone marrow.

As a young boy staying at my Grandmother Carrie Rice's house on occasion, I'd sleep in the east bedroom. "The room Bert stayed in for most of a year, as he recovered," my grandmother would sometimes tell me. He missed all or most of a school year at Liberty High.

It was believed that things like carrots and sunshine were good for that affliction. My Aunt Margie tells me my grandmother grew a lot of carrots, and that the family would fix a pallet outside in the sun for Bert to lay on, where he exposed his affected leg to soak up those healing rays.

He did mostly get over Osteomyelitis, but always walked with a limp. He was a patriot, but the disability kept him from the military. I never, though, heard him utter one word of complaint, or seek not to work because of it. Starting later in life, he managed LSU's Idlewild agricultural experiment station just out of Clinton, and retired from there. In season, he brought peaches to our home.

He always supported me. Sometimes instead of teasing me like others might, he'd gently chide me for something, but always in a gentlemanly way. When I bought this newspaper, he was among the first to subscribe, never having previously taken the Wilk-Amite Record. When I wrote something, I was mindful Uncle Bert would be reading it.

At some funerals, it's pretty obvious the pastor didn't know the person very well, and struggles with what to say. Listening to Reverend Burnie Schmidt, though, I could tell that wasn't the case. He talked about the legacy my uncle left, and how important it is to leave something good for your family and friends.

Recently, I was in Clinton at a business meeting. As is my custom when meeting someone from there, I asked the man if he knew my Uncle Bert Rice. He said: "I didn't know him very well, I only met him personally once, but I'll never forget what he did."

"One hot summer day in our early teens, a friend of mine and I had pedaled our bikes out the road where the Idlewild station is. We'd overextended ourselves in the heat, had nothing to drink, and were walking our bikes, way past ready to be back home."

"Your uncle came along, stopped, told us who he was, and told us to put our bikes in the back of the truck and hop in. He drove us to Clinton. I never dealt with him again, but have never forgotten the good thing he did."

Legacy. I think of Reverend Schmidt's words. If each of us left a legacy of just one random act of kindness as the way someone remembered us, wouldn't it be a better world?

Thank you, Uncle Bert, for the way you served your God, your family, and mankind. Surely you will dwell in the house of the Lord forever.


**INSURING THAT YOU SAVE A BUCK**

Growing up in Southwest Mississippi in a family that often had to "make do" financially taught me the value of being frugal. Car insurance costs were something my father and mother were careful about.

At the time, I didn't fully appreciate the fact they carried me on their auto insurance until I graduated from LSU, when I headed for the real world. Leaving school in the mid-1960s for the Air Force, I opted to obtain my own insurance with a company that specialized in covering military members.

Forty-nine years later, I'm still insured with that same company, and generally assume I'm getting a good enough deal. We've had a difference of opinion on two or three matters across the years, but overall I'm happy with them, and now carry our home insurance there as well.

But it pays to question why my company doesn't sometimes offer the discounts that others do, and when I see something new in the market, I write a letter or make a phone call and ask about it.

Are you hunkered down with one company and not alert to discounts that others offer? Bankrate.com recently looked at discounts offered by auto insurance companies and provided the following information. Here are just some discounts offered.

Daytime running lights: Four of the 10 largest companies offer discounts for these.

Low mileage: About 80% of insurers offer discounts for low mileage. They may provide a tracking device that will report actual miles driven.

Grades: Have a student in your family? His or her good grades may help with policy cost.

Occupation: Companies believe that people in certain occupations or those who spend a lot of time on the road may be less likely to take risks.

Alumni associations and clubs: Certain of these have teamed with insurance companies to offer discounts to members. Check with your insurer for affiliate groups, or with your organization.

Multiple polices: Having homeowner, auto, and life insurance through one company can earn you a substantial discount.

Does your vehicle have an antitheft system or environmentally friendly component? Even tinted windows may help you. You may also qualify for customer loyalty, paperless billing, paying your whole bill at once, being a current or former military member, or having a newer model car.

You may qualify for a discount if you have more cars than you can drive. After all, you can only drive one at a time, so your insurer has no risk when the other one is sitting still.

I have a shop in another state and though I don't have a vehicle stored there now, in the past I've kept an extra vehicle, usually an old truck, to use when there temporarily. Recently I learned that my insurance company allows me to have my extra vehicle in storage or inactive status, but to have it insured while infrequently there just by calling them and telling them of my beginning and ending dates of usage. That's given me substantial savings, but I let a lot of years go by before I found out about it.

Of course, being a safe driver nearly always provides better rates. Do yourself a favor and look into these discounts. Times are tough enough and you may be pleasantly surprised how you can save some money.

## EATING AWAY AT US

I grew up a skinny Amite County kid. Food had no special appeal, except at holidays like Thanksgiving. Inside my head still lives that skinny kid, but I'm shocked when I see a current "wrong angle" picture.

While a boy, I was taught to clean my plate. "Think about those starving kids in China," we were told.

As a junior at LSU, I decided to gain weight, and between joining a gym, and eating specifically for that purpose, 25 pounds were added in 90 days. They're still attached.

At 6'1" tall, my Air Force "fighting weight" for 28 years was 212 pounds. An annual mandatory weigh-in helped. But lately, I'd crept up to 240 pounds. Too many.

More recently, I've lost 10, mostly by eating only two meals a day, one at mid-morning, then supper before 5 pm. When a nighttime hunger pain strikes, a glass of water helps. But yesterday I was bad, and the scale was up two pounds today.

Just wanted you to know I fight my own battles before I say what follows. Last Saturday, headed away from Gloster, I stopped at a Cracker Barrel. And no, it wasn't in Mississippi. As I looked around, America's problem with obesity came into full focus.

Cracker Barrel advertises comfort food, and wow, am I comfortable there. I also listen to audio books while I travel, and rent from those stores.

Only one table out of 20 had more "normal" size people than fat. To my right sat a very big man, alone. I'd swear he was salivating as his food was served. If a Doberman pinscher sized up my leg the same way, I'd be fearful of my life.

To my left sat a grandmother, grandfather, daughter, and grandson. The grandmother was a little overweight, but the others made up for her in a big way. Besides the fact he was a real whiner, the three year old boy was obviously too heavy. What chance does he have?

In front were two women and a man, all way too large. One woman brazenly wore a shirt that read: "I'm not fat, I'm just fluffy." If I wasn't seeing a lot of fat, I sure was seeing an enormous amount of fluff.

The problem extended to Cracker Barrel's servers, at least half of them overweight. Two young women were especially so. One perspired heavily just walking around, and I truly felt sorry for her. How tough it must be to carry all that food and stare at it in the process.

I'm no Dr. Phil, thank goodness, but I suspect eating is something we can control as individuals and with so many problems with such as government, family, and jobs, many of us just let 'er rip, and our clothes, as a consequence, do the same. When someone displays a message like the "fluffy" one, probably that person has given up.

Given up to problems like diabetes, broken-down knees, hips, feet, etc., and a painful older age. What a shame.

Christians condemn those who commit certain sins, but often we conveniently overlook overeating. What does our Bible say? Here's some examples. Proverbs 23:20-21: "Do no join those who drink too much wine or gorge themselves on meat, for drunkards and gluttons become poor, and drowsiness clothes them in rags." Proverbs 28:7: "He who keeps the law is a discerning son, but a companion of gluttons disgraces his father."

If you're already feeling uncomfortable, skip this one. Proverbs 23:2 proclaims: "Put a knife to your throat if you are given to gluttony". Ouch!


## NEXT YEAR

I'm Mississippi to the bone. Born in Amite County. My first years through age 12 were in Liberty. My family and I were always Ole Miss Rebel fans.

Living in Oregon, Arizona, Texas, and New Mexico in later years, my loyalty has always been to Mississippi, my home state.

In 1957, my dad gravitated to booming Baton Rouge for work. By 1959, I was a 10th grader at Istrouma High School. Billy Cannon had been a football star there. His aunt was one of my teachers. At Istrouma, it was a given you'd go to LSU if you went to college at all. Billy, of course, was LSU's star running back.

On Halloween Day, October 31st, 1959, I was under a pecan tree polishing my 1949 Chevy, bought new in Liberty by Mr. Sedgie Boyd, and bought used by me from Bryant Jones on Liberty's Main Street. My AM car radio was on the LSU-Ole Miss game. Both schools were unbeaten. When Billy Cannon made that run to win the game for LSU by 7 to 3 - still called The Game by many in Louisiana - I guess it was a turning point.

Until then my loyalties had been confused. But a tiny little thing fell out of the tree and landed on my shoulder that day. It was a microscopic tiger. After that, I'd root for Ole Miss - but not if they were playing LSU.

On Saturdays, my first cousin George Rice, a year younger, and I would take a city bus to Tiger Stadium, and sell Cokes at the game to get in. Not much later, he was an All-American playing defensive tackle at LSU, followed by five years in the NFL. George, who was also born in Liberty, was sort of the Barney Poole of Baton Rouge.

Attending LSU from 1961 - 1965, I was always broke. I worked 30 hours weekly at Baton Rouge General Hospital or at Holiday Inn on Airline Highway, next door to the - yes - Tiger Drive-In. Ecstasy was an unpunched $10 meal ticket at a LSU-area café. Vienna sausage and Ramen Soup were more the norm. I lived in the cheapest dorm at LSU, North Stadium, underneath that concrete monstrosity. Death Valley isn't so much the name of the football field now as it was the name of my home back then.

My roommates and I were 300 feet from Mike the Tiger's cage, and were jealous of the meat fed to Mike. We wondered how we might get into his cage and take some. Nothing, I think, steels your loyalties and character like poverty.

"Ole Miss" week at LSU was something else. The Baton Rouge Fire Department sent trucks out to hose us down, cool us off.

I'm always surprised how much support there is now in Southwest Mississippi for LSU. It hasn't always been that way.

Ole Miss fans will love to read this, but that 27 to 24 LSU loss was a tough one. I confess that Ole Miss played harder and smarter and deserved to win, but that didn't help me much.

And I'm not a fanatical football fan, believe me. After a couple of recovery days, I've accepted last Saturday's 27-24 loss.

Like the country song says, everyone wants to go to heaven but nobody wants to go today. Just in case, I've confessed my sins to the Good Lord already. So you can bet your sweet bippy that if I'm on my deathbed anytime soon, and someone overhears my dying declaration, it may not be what you expect but something like this instead:

"Just…wait…until…next…year…"

# Chapter 20

# NUCLEAR SKEETERS

## 'PICING' ON MOSQUITOES

BACK HOME AFTER more than 50 years, I've found many changes but also something that hasn't. Mosquitoes.

If you grow up in Mississippi and/or Louisiana, you take them for granted. In high school in Baton Rouge in the 1950s/1960s, drive-in theatres were also a fixture. They were the Motel 6 of the day, where someone left the light off - not on - for us. And mosquitoes, as if hired by your date's parents, were always determined to interfere.

No self-respecting teenager took his girlfriend to a drive-in movie without his "Pic, #14 pocket size, Repels mosquitoes, Q-U-I-C-K!, also gnats and sand flies". In a box that was yellow and black and red, they sold for 29 cents. One nostalgia buff recalls them this way:

"Pic was a burning coil… A light, aluminum stand held the incense-like coil aloft. You lit the end and it emitted a wonderful, near incense-like odor. It kept the 'skeeters away. The coil burned very slowly and evenly. One could monitor its progress, see when the ash was ready to knock off. This brings back wonderful flashes from my youth. Oh, to smell that again! As I recall, it worked pretty well, too."

A "Pic", looking like a small green electric stove coil, was a drive-in necessity. Let's say one arrived home and your mother or dad saw mosquito bites in questionable places. There was some 'splaining to do, and you wished you'd spent the 29 cents. I burned my share of Pics at the Tiger Drive-In on Airline Highway in Baton Rouge.

Leaving for the Air Force after LSU graduation, I'd gotten a newer car. My Pic was an indispensable piece of survival gear and I couldn't imagine life without it, so it moved to the new glove compartment. While not Pic-addicted, I was Pic-dependent. Do you believe in miracles? Arriving in Tucson, Arizona, at Davis-Monthan AFB, it was just amazing to find - no mosquitoes!

There were also no trees, no green grass, no moss, no rivers or lakes or ponds or rain or mud of any consequence. No crawfish, even. Just cactus. No self-respecting mosquito would live in such a place.

A favorite Tucson activity was attending drive-in movies in a pickup parked backwards, chairs set up in the bed. The absence of mosquitoes was unbelievable. As strange as it sounds, that stands out as a first discovery in leaving home and finding "there was a different world out there" from ours in Mississippi and Louisiana.

That little Pic traveled with me for 15 or 20 years, though. Pic dependence doesn't go away easily. The green coil finally disintegrated, just crumbled.

But mosquitoes later welcomed me on arrival in Texas, especially to the coast. If you hear that the first rodeo ever was in Pecos, Texas, on July 4th, 1883, not true. Long before that, anyone who could stay away from a mosquito for 8 seconds near the Gulf of Mexico was some kind of rodeo champion!

Seadrift, Texas, southwest of Houston, was a place I visited regularly. At night, you had to run from your car to a motel room office. If you accidentally let a mosquito in, the desk clerk just might refuse to rent you a room.

Later, living in New Mexico at an altitude of 9,000 feet, mosquitoes were strangely absent again. Seems they don't like cold weather. Back Home in the South now, I've been reintroduced to my old friends. Where's my Pic when I need it? Gone to dust. But my Off or something equivalent is usually close at hand.

Mosquitoes bring to mind something that happened in the Bible, or didn't happen, I ought to say. Why in heaven's name didn't Noah go ahead and swat those first two that strolled aboard the Ark?

## BOMBS AWAY

"I love this country, it's the government I'm afraid of." Anonymous…

We Southwest Mississippians love our country, and we're patriotic. We were raised to respect our government. We were taught we should believe those in charge.

Our government of, by, and for the people - theoretically - sometimes thinks it's smarter than the people it governs, and doesn't tell us everything. Maybe that's the case with the Roswell incident in 1947 which may have involved aliens. It's not always clear who decides what we should or shouldn't know. But President Truman said the buck stopped at the top.

During the summer of 1961, I worked at Larto Lake, Louisiana.

In January that year, I was just a fat, happy, dumb teenager finishing high school in Baton Rouge, getting ready to attend LSU. Well, I was actually skinny, but you know what I mean.

Information just coming out says that 1961 almost started off with a bang. A very big bang. We had no clue, did we?

Had it happened, our lives might have been a whole lot different, or even non-existent, depending on where you lived, or even which way the wind blew.

Information obtained through the Freedom of Information Act, available after 50 years have passed, informs us that the U.S. Air Force nearly detonated an atomic bomb over North Carolina on January 23, 1961. It would have been 260 times more powerful than the device that destroyed Hiroshima, Japan.

A B-52 bomber crash near Goldsboro, North Carolina, saw two Mark 39 hydrogen bombs break up in mid-air. Three of eight crew members died in the aircraft accident.

The report said one of the two bombs behaved exactly as a nuclear weapon is designed to function in wartime and that only a single low-voltage switch prevented detonation. Millions would have been killed in the initial blast which would have had the explosive power of four million tons of TNT.

Fallout could have been deposited over Washington, Baltimore, Philadelphia and New York City. Parker Jones, a senior engineer in the Sandia National Laboratories in Albuquerque, NM, wrote in a 1969 report that "one simple, dynamo-technology, low voltage switch stood between the United States and a major catastrophe".

Literally millions of lives were saved when thankfully one safety mechanism was initiated. As it turned out, the other three failed to work properly, possibly allowing for an unintended detonation. The bomb hit the ground, and a firing signal was sent to the bomb's nuclear core, making that one switch the only thing stopping near apocalyptic conditions.

With one wrong zap, with one less safety measure, the security controls would have been rendered useless. Luckily, one hydrogen bomb fell into a field near Faro, North Carolina, and the other simply tumbled into a meadow off Big Daddy's Road to be lost in history and paperwork, until now.

In 2012, the state of North Carolina placed a historical plaque at the site, describing a nuclear incident that took place in 1961.

It's funny what happened that our government never told us about. Kind of makes you wonder what might be going on now that we aren't aware of!

## A FOGGY RECOLLECTION

Launched in life from Dr. Butler's clinic on Main Street in Liberty, next to the barber shop, the next few years were spent as a child in Amite County before moving away. Essentially I would be gone more than 50 years before returning during 2011 and 2012 when the Wilk Amite Record was purchased.

In the long meantime, life showed me many things "out there". The recent WAR newspaper story about North Korean missiles brought back a memory. Vandenberg Air Force Base in California was mentioned as a place where anti-missile tests are being conducted today.

LSU's ROTC program had me as a member and I was commissioned as an officer in the US Air Force at graduation. I served over a 28 year period. One of my Air Force trips in the 1980s took me to Vandenberg AFB, on the California coast north of Los Angeles.

I was there for a two week course in international politics. Early one morning we were scheduled to wake up about 3 AM and observe a missile launching over the Pacific test range. By 4 AM we were being transported to viewing stands about a quarter mile from the launch site. Pretty exciting stuff!

Our bus was enveloped by thick fog coming in from the ocean. The drive to the site seemed risky but we arrived safely. On the reviewing stands, we could only see heavy fog. It was tough to see 10 feet. Launch time was 5 AM. We hoped the fog would clear. It didn't matter to the missile but it mattered to us.

At the appointed time, we heard the tremendous noise across the short distance but all we could see was – fog, fog, fog. Not even the glow of the powerful rocket engine was visible!

We were informed that the test was successful. For all we knew, they had played a recording of a missile launch on giant loudspeakers though I certainly do believe a rocket was sent away. My memory of that whole episode is now humorous and somewhat - yes – foggy.

Just all part of the world I found beyond Amite County!

# Chapter 21

RESPECT THE SOLDIER

## CONFEDERATE MONUMENTS

THIS IS WRITTEN contemporary with the publication of this book in 2017.

Many in today's society advocate rewriting history by the destruction or hiding of monuments that mark Civil War history. The Confederate monument in Liberty, Mississippi, has been a part of the landscape of my life since I was a child.

Nine Anders soldiers gave their lives in that cause. I know none of my forbearers who were slave owners. I believe like any of us would have, they were simply attempting to protect their land, their homes, their families. And there was intense public pressure from your friends and neighbors to serve.

*Confederate memorial monument in Liberty, Mississippi, dedicated in 1871, honors 279 Amite County men who gave their lives.*

It was your duty.

The South lost the war and everyone knows that. But history

does not go away because someone doesn't like it. To rewrite events by tearing down things is wrong. That dishonors my family and other families whose relatives gave their lives.

Southerners have bucked up without complaint and have done their duty since, as honorable, law-abiding citizens of the United States of America. The memorial on the Liberty Courthouse lawn attests to the fact that many Amite Countians have given their very lives in defense of our country. There are hundreds and maybe even a few thousand county men and women who have served during both war and peace.

My Uncle Bill Rice for whom I'm named was a member of the U. S. 8th Air Force in England during WWII. Many of my relatives – uncles, cousins and others – have been members of the U. S. military.

Yours truly volunteered for Southeast Asia during the Vietnam War. I was sent to Thailand where I spent one year. Altogether I served 28 years in the U. S. Air Force, retiring as a Lieutenant Colonel. My call up notice for service in the first Gulf War came to my home but that conflict was over before I could be mobilized.

My point is – we pull our weight in your behalf. Please respect Southern history and leave Confederate monuments in place. They're there to honor war dead, men who gave their all. They're not there to fight the Civil War over again.

Focus instead on accounts like the following one. It's the story of a cousin who lost his life in Italy during WWII. He's just

242

one example of those who sacrificed his own future to give you one, and this is what real men do. They don't complain about history, they do what is necessary in the present.

**THE SOLDIER ON THE MANTLE**

To me, in my childhood, he was simply the Soldier on the Mantle.

The mantle wasn't in a sad home. But I wondered about the photo of the man in uniform, and my one question about him, when I was about seven, was met with sadness.

"Who's that?" I'd asked. "That was Albert," my Great Aunt Fannie told me. "He died in the war." WWII. Somehow I came to believe he'd died in France during the Normandy invasion.

Many people have soldiers on the fireplace mantle. Perhaps you do. Maybe yours served in later wars, like Vietnam, Iraq or Afghanistan. Maybe they're your sons or grandsons. Could be they're young women.

Fortunately, most come home safely. I hope yours did, or do. Their service is appreciated. They're the reason we live in a free country.

Aunt Fannie was an "old maid" until age 50. But Albert's mother died, and somehow Mr. Neyland and my aunt met and married. Thus my aunt became Albert's stepmother. They farmed and ranched way out in the Mississippi boonies.

Going there was through a gap, up and over a hill, down into a hollow where there was a creek bed, through another gap, then up another long hill to their home. It may have been a mile off the main road. Maybe it was only a quarter of a mile and another three-fourths mile of faulty memory. It's been 40 years since my last visit.

A gap? In some places they call them a wire gate. It's a temporary gate, really. Just an opening in the fence closed with a collection of wires and sticks.

Temporary? A friend once said the most permanent structure on a farm was a temporary barn. Gaps are like that. They stay a long time. In my youth, the youngest occupant who was physically able to handle the gap exited the car, opened and closed it. Gap duty.

That's why gapsters always campaigned for a little brother or sister, I suppose.

But going to my Uncle Wiley's and Aunt Fannie's house was fun. Surprisingly, they were among the first to have television. So we visited on Saturdays when the best TV shows were on.

There, like birds on a wire, we'd line up on the couch and watch the Hit Parade, I Led 3 Lives, the Loretta Young Show. I remember Loretta swishing in through a door in the opening scene, her full evening dress flying around in a circle. The Soldier on the Mantle silently watched with us. Though still curious about him, I kept quiet.

There were other things I liked there. A Dodge truck, a Ford tractor, two horses, and a spring. The backyard was full of turkeys, some of the toms mean, and I didn't like them. They'd chase you. Annually, a couple of the meanest ones were Guests of Honor at Thanksgiving.

When one was in pursuit, it made you feel better to know you'd be eating him later, something the turkey didn't seem to understand.

The Soldier had driven that Dodge truck or that Ford tractor, or similar ones, before he left for Army training in 1943. Horses live a long time so he may have ridden them, too.

Once my first wife and I were visiting, and she was petting a horse. They were friendly, but were seldom ridden, and then by someone they knew. "Suppose I could ride one?" she asked. "Of course. See how gentle they are," I said. So she hopped up on one, bareback. The horse, insulted, promptly bucked her off.

Not one to curse, nevertheless she shouted: "You SOB!" as she flew by me horizontally, Superwoman-style. And her comment wasn't for the horse. I still recall getting The Look. I think it was all mentioned later in divorce court.

All this has been sitting on a brain shelf for a very long time. Recently, researching old newspaper articles in Mississippi for a project, I glanced at a paper dated October 1, 1948, and noticed the following:

"Funeral services were held for Albert G. Neyland at the Presbyterian Church Tuesday afternoon, September 28, the pastor, Reverend I. O. Alexander, officiating, assisted by Dr. C. M. Savage, pastor of the Baptist Church.

Albert, the son of Mr. Wiley Neyland and the late Mrs. Neyland, was killed in action at or near Casino, Italy, January 14, 1944. He entered the service of our country May 3, 1943. He was 21 years of age, that age when life is looked forward to as a glorious future, but he paid the supreme sacrifice for his country.

He was born and raised in Liberty and attended school here, so it is fitting that he rest in peace here. He was a member of the Presbyterian Church, having accepted Christ as Savior early in life.

He is survived by his father and stepmother of Liberty, two brothers, Harry and Carl and one sister, Bonnie, all of Baton Rouge, three nephews and one niece, also of Baton Rouge.

Military rites were conducted at the graveside, sweet and impressive."

By pure chance I learned more about the Soldier than I'd ever known. He was killed in Italy, not France, just prior to four great battles the Allies fought to advance north past the great hilltop abbey of Monte Casino, built in AD524. The first such battle officially started January 17, 1944. The Germans had put up stiff resistance beforehand as Allied forces moved into place.

Why was his funeral service held in 1948 when he was killed in action during 1944? My guess is that his body was buried in Italy, later exhumed and returned to the United States for proper services.

It's as if the Soldier on the Mantle found a way to speak after all this time. I wish he knew he was remembered, even years ago by a young boy who silently wondered about his fate. I wish he'd come home safely to eat those Thanksgiving turkeys with us, since they'd probably chased him too.

There was always a mental place for him at the table, although it was never talked about.

*Chapter 22*

# FINIS

**THANK YOU**

LIBERTY'S LITTLE RED Schoolhouse was chosen for the cover. That's certainly not an original thought but nothing symbolizes Amite County, Mississippi, any better. Sixty years ago, during 1957, my family returned from Oregon to the South, settling in Baton Rouge. My sister and I spent that summer in Liberty with our grandparents. She was off to college in the fall but I started the 9th grade temporarily in Liberty pending transfer to a Louisiana school.

For that one month, I attended classes in the Little Red Schoolhouse, downstairs. My initials may be carved there somewhere but sometimes it's better not to look! After all, I was a young boy with a pocketknife. Thank goodness the building was saved those many years ago, and that it is so well maintained today. It's another reason for my gratitude to the Amite County Historical and Genealogical Society.

Thank you for reading my book. My hope is that family, friends and others have learned something about my birthplace. Amite County, Mississippi, gave me a wonderful start in life and has always been a place to be proud of. It will always be my real home. May God bless each of you as He has blessed me!

CPSIA information can be obtained
at www.ICGtesting.com
Printed in the USA
LVHW05s0044120418
573172LV00002BC/4/P